Cricket Cartoons
AND CARICATURES

The MCC CRICKET LIBRARY

Cricket Cartoons
AND CARICATURES

·GEORGE PLUMPTRE·

WILLOW BOOKS
Collins
8 Grafton Street, London w1
1989

To E.W.S.

Willow Books
William Collins Sons & Co Ltd
London · Glasgow · Sydney · Auckland
Toronto · Johannesburg

First published 1989
© MCC and George Plumptre 1989

BRITISH LIBRARY CATALOGUING IN PUBLICATION DATA
Plumptre, George
Cricket cartoons and caricatures.
1. English cartoons. Special subjects
Cricket to 1988
I. Title
741.5'942

ISBN 0-00-218317-X

Set in Sabon by
Rowland Phototypesetting Ltd
Bury St Edmunds, Suffolk
Originated, printed and bound by
C. S. Graphics Pte, Singapore

Contents

List of Illustrations

(Page references in bold refer to colour plates)

Introduction

This book was conceived and produced under the auspices of the MCC, in conjunction with the publishers, Collins Willow. As a result, not only has it been written from the standpoint of Lord's and the MCC, but the caricatures and cartoons around which it is written have been drawn primarily from the MCC's collection at Lord's. It was never intended that the book would be the definitive work on cricket caricature and cartoon, but rather an anthology, and while its text attempts in places to give as broad a coverage of the subject as possible, its pictorial material is essentially selective.

As with the club's other works of art, the MCC is extremely fortunate in its collection of caricatures and cartoons, built up over many decades. One point of particular importance is that the club holds many of the original drawings, sketches or watercolours from which the printed versions were taken – inevitably losing some quality in the process. Therefore, for this book, we have tried as far as possible to use original material to maintain an overall level of quality. Nothing makes the point more clearly than to see Spy's delightful watercolour sketch for a *Vanity Fair* cartoon which previously one had seen only as a neat and amusing but somewhat lifeless print.

Availability of original material has been one factor in the inclusion or absence of pictures or artists from the book. Perhaps a more basic feature is that the book's strengths, in terms of its contents, to a certain extent reflect those of the MCC. There is no doubt that the club has some of the most exquisite – and valuable – cricket caricatures and cartoons ever produced, such as Thomas Rowlandson's cartoon of a ladies' match from 1811 and some original pen and ink drawings by nineteenth-century *Punch* artists.

Inevitably, though, there are gaps and it is to fill the most important of these that I have drawn on material from outside

the MCC's collection. For instance, a book on cricket caricature and cartoon – however selective it professes to be –
without a cartoon by Tom Webster, of whose work the MCC
does not hold any original material, would not be complete.

As far as the arrangement of the text and pictures into
chapters is concerned, I felt that it was important to give in the
first chapter an overview of the historical development of the
game alongside that of English caricature and cartoon. Without this – even in the most basic terms – it is difficult to
appreciate and understand the interplay between the two and
how they evolved and changed over time. Thereafter the
chapters are selective and reflect to some extent the nature of
the material to be included among the illustrations, but they
have been organised to cover some of the richer sources of
humorous cricketing art.

Taken overall the pictures show, first, what a productive
source of artistic humour the game of cricket has been, and
second, what a strong part of the English social fabric it has
become. They also give a clear indication of attitudes towards
the game at different times and how these changed from one
period to another.

Although revealing about the game of cricket and its public
reception, the pictures are less often revealing about the men
who drew them. It is surprising to discover how many caricaturists and cartoonists, producing material of wit or hilarity as
a daily routine, have been serious, self-effacing, and sometimes melancholy or even depressive. They have often been
men of acute social conscience, which at times gives a note of
poignancy to the humour of their work. Without exception
the most successful have been supreme observers, and their
effectiveness has lain in a simple or obvious idea.

George Plumptre
March 1989

CHAPTER ONE

Historical Progress

The relationship between cricket and caricature has produced a uniquely rich vein of humour among English sports. This is not altogether surprising for, more than any other of our sporting pastimes, cricket has attracted the attention of artists, writers and a host of other observers and commentators.

For over two centuries cricket has been evolving steadily through stages, from a basic game to a national institution. It is the attainment of this institutional status which has been fundamental in the game's attraction for humorous artists. By the mid to late nineteenth century not only had cricket become recognized as something peculiarly English in both the way it was played and its philosophy, it was also part of the national identity. In 1945 when the cartoonist David Low depicted the leaders of Britain, America, Russia and France in national sporting attire, it was inevitable for Churchill to be in cricket whites.

Crucial to the game's appeal to caricaturists and cartoonists has been the manner in which cricket has offered a potential beyond the purely sporting. It has provided an ideal backdrop for social comment and political images. Indeed, in the game's early days it was primarily political scenes that were used to illustrate cartoons. Thereafter, as the game grew and spread – not only within England but to the outposts of the Empire and beyond – and its leading players became household names, the variety of subject matter increased accordingly.

It is therefore logical to begin by sketching the simultaneous development of the two traditions, and this has been done from the standpoint of cricket's headquarters and premier institution – Lord's ground and the Marylebone Cricket Club.

For it was largely as a result of the authority and status which the ground and club were to achieve and maintain during the nineteenth century that cricket assumed the importance it did and the players their lofty reputations.

It is a happy coincidence that 1787, the year of the MCC's official formation, was a time when the country was enjoying what has come to be called the Golden Age of English Caricature. It was a period ushered in around the middle of the eighteenth century by William Hogarth and his incisive satirical commentaries upon life at that time, the most famous of which are his illustrations such as 'Marriage à la Mode' and 'The Rake's Progress'. By the last quarter of the century hand-coloured prints, usually sold direct from the shops of a series of London publishers, had become the most accepted and popular style of illustrating – and, more often than not, ridiculing – the major events and personalities of the day. Hogarth's successors fed the appetite of a public which delighted in the spectacle of the more grotesque side of human activity, and for whom politicians, royalty and other public figures were legitimate targets for derision and rudery.

Today it is impossible fully to appreciate the caricatures of this period without understanding the background of English life which produced them. Most later generations have at times found them too savage or repugnant. Nevertheless, it was their uninhibited vigour and style which formed the foundation of the modern cartoon and caricature, and no subsequent period has achieved the strength of satire that was seen between the accession of George III in 1760 and that of his son, sixty years later.

The caricatures were true to their age in the range of features they combined. As well as the pure quality of draughtsmanship, the effect of which was increased by the deeply cut lines of the etchings from which the prints were taken, they were full of imagination, wicked malevolence, rollicking vulgarity, sexual innuendo, a balance of dry wit and earthy humour and, at times, even revolting images. All of these were a natural part of life in late Georgian England.

Foremost among the artists was James Gillray, the greatest of all English caricaturists. Gillray's career began in earnest during the 1780s and for the next twenty-five years, until his obsession with failing eyesight and his heavy drinking produced bouts of madness, he satirized and depicted the leading personalities of the day with merciless incision and supreme power. At home, the royal family and politicians – especially William Pitt the Younger and Charles James Fox – provided him with endless inspiration, while abroad, the horrors of the French Revolution produced his most macabre images and strongly influenced the public's view of the Paris mob, the revolutionary leaders and later Napoleon.

For most of his career Gillray worked for Mrs Hannah Humphreys, a leading print-seller, and lived above her shop in St James's Street. It was here, after two years of almost total confinement, that he died in 1815. The unassailable reputation that he had achieved is confirmed by one of his twentieth-century admirers and successors, David Low: 'From the infantile, incoherent and fitful state of caricature after Hogarth, Gillray fashioned for himself a medium that ... caused England to become known as the House of Caricature.'

To Gillray, political satire was a serious business and he almost always showed specific people rather than 'types'. For him, the game of cricket had not yet assumed sufficient importance, either in its own right or as a source of imagery, to provide suitable subject matter. Quite different, however, was the attitude of Thomas Rowlandson, another leading artist of the time, who had been born in the same year as Gillray.

Rowlandson's lifestyle was typical of the times, with constant drinking, gambling and other heavy spending, and resulting impecuniousness. But his prodigious talent as an artist was clear at an early age and his developing skill as a draughtsman, combined with his humorous approach to life, provided the foundations of his work as a caricaturist. Although he did produce much political satire, Rowlandson's work was just as often witty social comment or illustration of scenes from English life.

One of the latter was the still youthful game of cricket, and in 1790 he drew 'Cricket in White Conduit Fields', in pen and watercolour. White Conduit Fields in Islington was the place where, as members of the White Conduit Club, those aristocrats who made up the earliest members of the MCC had first played their cricket. In 1787 they decided to move to a ground of their own, first to Dorset Square, subsequently in 1811 to North Bank, Regent's Park and finally, in 1814, to the site of the present ground, named – as the other two had been – after their attendant who had acquired each of the grounds, Thomas Lord.

So cricket was beginning to attract the attention of the leading artists, although one cannot deny that, as is the case with an earlier picture of White Conduit Fields, drawn in 1784 by Robert Dighton, a contemporary watercolourist and caricaturist, Rowlandson's sketch is more an attractive view than a caricature. Within twenty years, however, there was a marked progression, as is shown in Rowlandson's 1811 drawing of a ladies' cricket match, which is illustrated and described in Chapter Four.

The mantle of Gillray and Rowlandson was taken on by their immediate successors working during the period of the Regency, in particular by George Cruikshank – the most outstanding member of a family of gifted engravers and artists – whose caricatures are highly evocative of the period. None the less things were beginning to change, and the bite of the late eighteenth century masters was becoming less evident. By the 1830s and the accession of the young Queen Victoria, England was fast becoming a different nation in both character and attitude. Fierce satire and rudery were becoming unacceptable, and in 1832 Gillray was condemned by the *Athenaeum* as 'a caterpillar on the green leaf of reputation'.

The stage was set for the arrival of a publication which was to typify and embody the standards of Victorian England:

Punch, whose first issue was published in 1841. For the rest of the century and beyond, *Punch* was central to the development of English humour and its influence can never be understated. The talents of the successive artists who worked for the magazine ensured that it acquired, for some decades at least, a virtual monopoly over caricature and cartoon. If by the end of the century the monopoly had been broken, most decisively by the challenge of national daily newspapers, *Punch* has still remained in the forefront ever since.

Punch's views and opinions were those of the swelling ranks of the Victorian middle classes. Its subject matter reflected their interests: politics, the Empire, society and sport. John Leech, the magazine's first leading artist who produced over 700 cartoons for *Punch* between 1841 and 1864, is best remembered for his hunting scenes. Simon Houfe commented in the *Dictionary of British Book Illustrators and Caricaturists 1800–1914* that 'his humour was like his talent, gentle, warm-hearted and positive, his world the ups and downs of middle-class life, the sports of the squirearchy and the peccadilloes of army officers and undergraduates'. The subdued nature of his humour, so different from that of his rumbustious predecessors, represented what Ruskin referred to as 'that great softening of the English mind'.

As the edges of the nation's humour became blunted, and *Punch* played a decisive role in this process, so the magazine gave caricature and cartoon a position as an accepted part of the establishment that would have been unthinkable in Gillray and Rowlandson's day. The extent to which this process continued through the century was confirmed in 1894 when John Tenniel, *Punch*'s leading artist since the 1860s, was awarded a knighthood. One can hardly imagine William Pitt or George III feeling so generously disposed towards a man who had pilloried them as mercilessly as Gillray had done.

At the same time as *Punch*'s star was moving rapidly into the ascendant, that of the game of cricket was following a similarly successful course. As far as Lord's and the MCC were concerned, crucial events during the preceding decades had been the safeguarding of the ground in 1825 when William Ward, banker and leading cricketer, had purchased the lease from Thomas Lord, and the establishment of the three fixtures which, at least until the advent of Test cricket during the 1880s, were to be the ground's foremost annual events, not only for the sport, but also for their social importance: Eton *v* Harrow (first played in 1805), Gentlemen *v* Players (first played in 1806) and Oxford *v* Cambridge (first played in 1827). As shall be seen later, these fixtures provided ideal material for the artists of *Punch* and other publications.

Meanwhile, cricket was spreading out rapidly from the centre which, in terms of authority and influence (MCC had drawn up and now controlled the game's *Laws*), Lord's had unquestionably become. Out in the provinces, the first stirrings were taking place by the middle of the century which were to lead to the establishment of county clubs and, during the 1890s, the start of the formal county competition. At a less exalted level, the game could be seen on an increasing number of village greens. These and other strands of development were clear indicators that cricket was becoming part of the fabric of English life. And as the trend of English caricature and cartoon moved towards a style of gentle, witty comment upon the country's traditions, so cricket became an increasingly suitable subject.

But no story is complete without a hero, and during the 1860s one such appeared upon cricket's horizon – W. G.

NEW CRICKETING DRESS
To protect all England against the present swift bowling
John Leech (1817–64)
1854. *Punch*

During the middle of the 19th century the Lord's wicket came under fire from all sides because it was uneven and dangerous. The problem was not alleviated until the ground was relaid in 1964.

LORD'S IN DANGER
The MCC go out to meet the enemy
E. T. Reed (1860–1933)
1891. *Punch*

Grace. Grace revolutionized the game's popularity, prestige and importance and was the first cricketer to become a national figure. By the end of the century he was as well known as Queen Victoria and Mr Gladstone.

Assessing Grace's phenomenal and unparalleled influence upon cricket one can only conclude that this came about through a combination of his ability at the game and the power of his personality, a combination that was summed up by Ronald Mason in *Barclays World of Cricket*:

By force of skill he made a well-established game into something infinitely varied and resourceful; by fortune of physique and energy of personality he presented to his country a transformed pastime, half spectacle and half science, with the power to entrap at times the imaginative sympathies of a whole nation.

In addition to his cricketing prowess and expansive character, Grace was a caricaturist's dream. His huge frame, which belittled the bat he used to such effect, the thick beard and shock of hair – as often as not topped with the striped cap of the MCC – were depicted more often than the features of any other single cricketer. Equally important, here was a figure with whom artists and the general public could immediately identify the game of cricket. A good example was a *Punch* cartoon which appeared in 1890, entitled 'Lord's in Danger' and showing Grace leading the MCC into battle against the Great Central Railway, which had promoted a bill in Parliament to gain possession of Lord's and lay a railway line through the ground.

In 1868, the year in which Grace began the career with his native county, Gloucestershire, that was to last for three decades, the first edition of *Vanity Fair* appeared. During the next thirty-odd years the magazine was to produce one of the best-known and most popular collections of cricket caricatures. Shortly after its publication, *Vanity Fair* rose to enormous popularity which it retained for most of its relatively short life, until ceasing publication under its own name in 1913. The artistic highlight was the weekly full-page colour caricature of a leading personality of the day. Selection as the subject was a considerable cachet and over the years 33 cricketers achieved the accolade. In addition, a handful of other cricketers were depicted in another guise, such as C. B. Fry who appeared as an athlete. Inevitably, W. G. Grace was the first cricketer to appear, in 1877.

During *Vanity Fair*'s years of greatest success – between 1870 and the turn of the century – most of the caricatures were drawn by three artists who between them gave a fascinating insight into the melting-pot of London's artistic life. First was Carlo Pellegrini, known as 'Ape', who was born at Capua in 1838, served as a soldier with Garibaldi and came to London in 1864. Pellegrini was once described by Frank Harris: 'In person he was a grotesque caricature of humanity, hardly more than five feet two in height, squat and stout, with a face like a mask of Socrates, and always curiously illdressed.'

The most prolific *Vanity Fair* artist was Spy, or Sir Leslie Ward, who was born in 1851 into an almost exclusively artistic family – both his father and grandfather were Royal Academicians and his mother was also an artist. Spy was an Old Etonian whose caricatures, although clever likenesses at times, lacked life or humour. His critics have always maintained that he was a compulsive snob and that the main attraction of his commissions was the contact it gave him with the great and famous.

Spy's bland likenesses to some extent reflected late Victorian and early Edwardian philosophy and humour. Flattering in a suitably subdued manner, while they often caused a smile they never brought forth anything so vulgar as a guffaw. At the same time as he was producing them, there was a certain air throughout the country of conceit and self-importance born of the Empire and Great Britain's industrial and commercial supremacy.

How different was the welcome return of sharp wit to caricature in the work of Max Beerbohm. Beerbohm signed himself simply Max, and his most incisive caricatures were of the artistic, literary and theatrical world of the 1890s in which he himself was a leading figure and whose personalities he knew intimately. His humour has often been described as puckish, which it certainly was, for he delighted in knocking people off pedestals in a manner often so subtle and disguised that the victim hardly noticed. Beerbohm drew a number of *Vanity Fair*'s weekly caricatures and they were probably the magazine's best, but it is a good indication of his reputation that Owen Seaman, *Punch*'s cautious editor at the time, thought his work dangerously sharp and never employed him.

There is no doubt that it was Max's wit, his acute powers of observation and his imagination that were the basis of his genius as a caricaturist, rather than his draughtsmanship. None the less, his exquisite style is instantly recognizable. His technique of extreme exaggeration recalled the masters of the late eighteenth century, Gillray and Rowlandson. In terms of the development of caricature Max's strong outlines, filled with washes usually of soft, pastel colours, marked a clear departure from the almost inevitable *Punch* style of dense pen and ink cross-hatching, which had been made the magazine's trademark by its longest-serving senior artist, John Tenniel, and was followed by the majority of his successors.

At the other end of the social scale from the inimitable Max a host of cheap, popular periodicals sprang up during the last quarter of the nineteenth century. Here the humour was refreshingly vigorous and vulgar, nowhere more so than in *Ally Sloper's Half Holiday*, a halfpenny weekly adored by thousands. The magazine's awful hero, Ally Sloper, with his carbuncle of a nose and stick-like legs with knobbly knees, was the creation of C. H. Ross. He was subsequently taken up by W. G. Baxter whose pictures of him are the most numerous and best known. Ally Sloper was a marvellous parody of the

English working class who loved him, with all his prejudices, patriotism and robustness.

The regularity with which Ally Sloper was to be found playing cricket or commenting on a cricket event of the moment confirmed as much as anything that the game had become truly popular. The firmness of its establishment and the breadth of its appeal now meant that it presented limitlessly varied opportunities for humorous artists to comment in their own particular way. We therefore have Spy's elegant and flattering portrayals of the game's heroes at the same time as *Punch*'s constant output on the theme of the duffer on the village green, and the ridiculous Ally Sloper's face leering out from between an Eton collar and topper amongst the 'toffs' at the Eton *v* Harrow match at Lord's.

Indeed, by the end of the nineteenth century cricket had embarked upon what has rightly been called its Golden Age. The 1880s had seen the beginning of Test cricket and the centenary of the MCC, the 1890s the completion of the present Lord's Pavilion and the formal establishment of the County Championship. A selection of the names who achieved greatness between 1890 and 1914, and whom posterity has invested with almost legendary reputations, suffices to recall the attractions of the period: MacLaren and Spooner, Ranji and Fry, Jackson, Jessop, Barnes, Hirst and Rhodes and, among the visitors from Australia, Noble, Gregory, Trumper and Hill.

If these giants of the game were heroes to the general public, they were also news. By the end of the nineteenth century this was a vital factor as the rise of national daily newspapers challenged the supremacy of *Punch* and other periodicals, not only for the attention of the reading public but also as the medium of caricature and cartoon. Built up into great institutions by the magnates of Edwardian England, the popular newspapers were to provide a whole new market for humorous art – in particular the cartoon. While it is certainly not true that *Punch* was eclipsed, or even that it suffered greatly from the rise of the popular daily, it could no longer claim the undisputed position as the senior organ of English caricature and cartoon that it had enjoyed since its foundation.

Fundamental to the development of the daily press and changes in cartoon style was progress in the printing process. The 1880s saw the beginning of the replacement of the wood-engraved blocks – invariably used in *Punch* – by the line

THREE OF A KIND
Tom Webster (1886–1962)
1933. *Daily Mail*

Producing a cartoon almost daily for over twenty years, Webster's work is unrivalled as humorous comment on the sporting world between the wars.

Elias 'Patsy' Hendren (1889–1962) was one of the game's great characters and it was no doubt partly his sense of humour which prompted him to appear against the West Indies in 1933 wearing a protective cap. As *Wisden* explained, 'Fashioned by his wife, this cap had three peaks, two of which covered the ears and temples, and which was lined with sponge rubber.'

YOU MAY RECALL SHEER READER THAT 'PATSY' HENDREN

OF MIDDLESEX IS WEARING 3 PEAKS TO HIS CAP AS A PROTECTION AGAINST LIVELY AND PROVOCATIVE CRICKET BALLS.

ALL THE CRICKET ENTHUSIASTS — THAT IS THE OLD GENTLEMEN OF LORDS — ARE ON FIRE ABOUT THIS. (THE FLAMES ARE ALREADY LICKING THE ROOF OF THE PAVILION.)

THE OLD GENTLEMEN OF LORDS SAY — AND QUITE RIGHTLY — THAT IF HENDREN HAS THREE PEAKS THEY WILL

HIP·HIP·HIP· HIP·HIP·HIP· HIP·HIP·HIP· AND ALL THE REST OF IT.

HAVE TO GIVE MORE THAN THREE CHEERS.

AND YOU NEVER KNOW WHERE THIS KIND OF THING IS GOING TO STOP. IF HENDREN CAN WEAR A CAP WITH THREE PEAKS HE MIGHT COME OUT

WITH THREE BATS IN WHICH CASE THE ———

— BOWLER MIGHT WANT TO DELIVER THREE BALLS AT

NINE STUMPS.

AND YOU ARE MISTAKEN IF YOU THINK WE HAVE RUN OUT OF HORRIBLE THOUGHTS. SUPPOSING THE UMPIRES WANT THREE TEA INTERVALS.

Left
A. E. TROTT (1873–1914)
Roland Hill. 'Rip'. (1873–1925)
1907

The various poses which Rip often showed his characters in – as in his pen and ink caricature of Albert Trott – can be seen as a simple introduction to the running cartoon later perfected by Tom Webster.

A. E. Trott was an Australian who played for his country but came to England and joined Middlesex after he was not picked for the 1896 side. His most famous moment came in 1899 when he hit a ball from his fellow Australian Monty Noble over the pavilion at Lord's, which accounts for Rip's caption.

block or half-tone block (the latter giving shades as well as outline). The mechanized printing process was far quicker, to the advantage of the dailies, and was soon to give them a decisive edge in illustrations with the reproduction of photographs, which became steadily easier and cheaper.

Coverage of sport was an essential ingredient of the national press and, initially in the absence of photographs, there was an immediate place for the cartoonist to provide illustrations to accompany articles and reports. The best of the early sports cartoonists was Roland Hill, or Rip, of the *Evening News*. In a sense, however, Rip's career – his style of cartoon and the annuals called *Kricket Karicatures* which he produced at the end of some seasons – paved the way for Tom Webster, who appeared shortly before the First World War and who during the 1920s and 1930s became the best sports cartoonist of all time.

Webster joined the *Daily Mail* in 1919, where he stayed until 1940. During that time he produced in the region of 5000 cartoons for the paper. His success was instantaneous and within a few years he was the highest-paid cartoonist in the world and an international celebrity. Webster remembered that the breakthrough he made in sports cartoons came partly as a result of the growing use of photography for

Right
UNCLE FRANK
'Uncle Frank, when you made that hundred against Yorkshire, was it with a hard ball?'
James Thorpe (1876–1949)
1934. *Punch*

James Thorpe lived most of his life in rural Hertfordshire where he found the scenes of club and village cricket which inspired much of his work. The MCC holds a large collection of original pen and ink drawings, many of which were done for his book *A Cricket Bag* (1929).

THE CHARM OF VILLAGE CRICKET.

THE CHARM OF VILLAGE CRICKET LIES TO A GREAT EXTENT IN THE STRESS IT PLACES ON THE INDIVIDUAL FACTOR.   FOR INSTANCE,
ONE KNOWS THAT, OTHER THINGS BEING EQUAL, IF ONE HITS THE BALL DIRECTLY TOWARDS A—

Fougasse

FIELDER IN A CLOTH CAP   AND IF HE'S WEARING BRACES   BUT IF HE'S GOT ON ONE OF   SIMILARLY, A BELT WITH A SNAKE
ONE CAN RUN A SINGLE —   ONE CAN RUN TWO—   THOSE FANCY SWEATERS ONE   IN IT MEANS A SINGLE—
                                                STAYS WHERE ONE IS.

SO DOES A CLUB   WHEREAS A GENT'S FANCY   ONE TAKES NO RISKS, OF   BUT ONE GETS IN TWO
TIE —   BOW MEANS TWO.   COURSE, WITH A HANDKER-   FOR TROUSERS TUCKED
                            CHIEF ROUND THE NECK—   INTO SOCKS—

STRETCHING IT TO THREE   AND FOUR FOR A BLACK   WHILE FOR CUFFS BUTTONED   OR A DICKEY ONE JUST
FOR A STRAW HAT —   WAISTCOAT—   AT THE WRIST—   RUNS IT OUT.

WITH SMALL BOYS IN SHORTS
ONE NATURALLY TAKES NO   AS EVERYONE KNOWS THEY ARE APT TO BECOME SO CONFOUNDEDLY ENTHUSIASTIC.
CHANCES WHATEVER—

THE CHARM OF VILLAGE
CRICKET
Cyril Kenneth Bird. 'Fougasse'
(1887–1965)
c. 1920

Fougasse first contributed to *Punch* in 1916. In 1937 he became art editor and, in 1949, editor, only the seventh in the magazine's history and the first artist to hold the position.

Fougasse's cartoon of village cricket is typical of much of his work; sparely drawn, linear figures whose style possibly owed much to his training as an engineer, an important balance between the drawings and captions, and the representation of character 'types'.

illustration, which meant that the cartoonist had to offer something more. 'I saw the red light, and realized that I had to find something the camera could not do, and at the same time I must appeal to the public. This then, was the genesis of the cartoon with the running comment. I exploited it for some time on the *Citizen* and won, I believe, a fair amount of success.'

Webster worked on the socialist *Daily Citizen* from 1912 until he left in 1914 to serve in the First World War. But it was with the *Daily Mail* that he perfected the technique of the cartoon with a running commentary, with which he is deservedly given the credit for revolutionizing sports cartoons. At a time when the daily newspapers were as yet unthreatened by radio or television, and when sport in general had never been more popular, Webster's impact upon both the general public and his medium was enormous.

Even if the circulation and readership of *Punch* had been threatened by the rise of the popular dailies, the challenge would have been well countered by the outstanding humorous artists whose work enlivened the pages of the magazine between the wars. That the magazine would contain plenty of material on cricket was ensured by the fact that, from 1919–37, the art editor was Frank Reynolds, a confirmed cricket enthusiast. His relish for the game was shared by James Thorpe, who with Reynolds was a member of the London Sketch Club, founded in 1898 and dominated by caricaturists and other artists. Thorpe's restrained and inoffensive cartoons appeared regularly in *Punch*, as had the work of Reynolds while an artist for the magazine before the war.

Both Reynolds and Thorpe were to a great extent traditional *Punch* artists in their style. Very different, however, was the work of three other men, all masters of the situation comedy which had now assumed great popularity in cartoon: Bateman, Fougasse and Pont. The social gaffe, the embarrassment of a poor innocent, or the archetypal English man or woman at their most comically typical – these were all situations which these three exploited continuously and brilliantly. For Bateman and Fougasse in particular (Fougasse's real name was Cyril Kenneth Bird and his father, Arthur Bird, had been an England cricketer), sport in general with cricket as a prominent ingredient was a major part of their repertoires.

In the cricket cartoons of these artists the people were

almost always 'types' – the club cricketer, the village batsman, the autograph-hunter, the solitary spectator etc. – but for Webster and the other artists who were depicting the major characters and events of the game, there was a feast of material. It was the period of Hobbs and Sutcliffe, Hendren, Woolley and Chapman, Larwood, Tate, Duleepsinhji and Hammond and, from Australia, the phenomenal Don Bradman. The two traditional Test opponents, Australia and South Africa, were joined by the West Indies, New Zealand and India, who played their first Test matches in England in 1928, 1931 and 1932 respectively. When the West Indians came in 1928 it was the start of the period which has seen Test cricket played in England during every subsequent summer (except for the years of the Second World War). People flocked in their thousands to watch cricket, and the Test matches were almost invariably full.

It was not as grand as during the Edwardian era, but first-class cricket was still played by gentlemen and players – as, indeed, it was until the 1960s – who had separate dressing-rooms and different gates on to the pitch. Morning dress was still worn at Eton v Harrow and the University Match. Social niceties were carefully observed both on and off the field, even if they were not universally enjoyed, and this was reflected in the way the game was depicted in caricature and cartoon.

The inter-war period saw a steady development towards the modern game of post-Second World War era. Overseas winter Test tours, although still lengthy operations due to the necessity of travelling by ship, were becoming a regular part of the annual cricket round, rather than the occasional expeditions they had been before the First World War. On the field itself the style of play was evolving towards what we are now used to, so that, to give a theoretical example, Bradman, Hammond or Tate would be technically more recognizable in a Test match today than, perhaps, MacLaren, Jessop or Rhodes might be.

After the enforced break of the Second World War there was a welcome continuity between the immediately pre-war years and the early ones after 1945, both among the leading players and among the artists who were illustrating cricket. At the same time, attendances at major matches were to swell during the post-war years, reaching their highest levels during the 1950s.

The 1960s saw many aspects of British social life which had

YORKSHIRE v VIETCONG
'I ain't heard nothing about a cricket
match between Yorkshire and the
Vietcong, have you Hank?'
Carl Giles. 'Giles'. (1916–)

One of the best-known post-war newspaper cartoonists, Giles has worked for
the *Daily* and *Sunday Express* since
1943. He has often produced cricket
cartoons at times when incidents have
been topical or newsworthy beyond the
confines of the game itself. One such
occasion occurred in 1967 when Yorkshire, under their indomitable captain
Brian Close, made themselves generally
unpopular for time-wasting in a match
against Warwickshire, thereby prevent-
ing their opponents from winning.

previously been accepted and taken for granted questioned,
threatened and at times rejected. The same happened in the
cricketing world, and the steady evolution of the game into an
overwhelmingly popular sport and an intrinsic part of the
country's social fabric seemed to check under scrutiny and, on
occasion, challenge.

The division between gentlemen and players had ended, the
unquestioned authority of the MCC was replaced with a
balance of power between the club and the newly formed Test
and County Cricket Board and National Cricket Association,
and the First-Class Counties were faced with the worrying
problem of having to become more commercial in the face of
declining attendances. In the international sphere the spectre
of anti-apartheid demonstrations in opposition to South
Africa appeared, raising the divisive and unsettling issue
which has plagued the game ever since.

All in all cricket was no longer charting the normally calm
waters it had become accustomed to in the past, and in the
1970s, just as England and Australia were celebrating the
centenary of Test cricket between the two countries, the most
dramatic challenge to the established game was thrown down
by the Australian Kerry Packer. Packer's alternative cricket
competitions may not have survived for long as an indepen-
dent offshoot, but he sent shock-waves through the game
which had a profound and lasting effect. However much the
traditionalists may not like it, there is no doubt that the
modern game as played in the 1980s shows the undeniable

effects of Packerism: the proliferation of one-day cricket, the huge roles of commercialism and the media, and the problems of maintaining any effective authority, either nationally or internationally.

As one would expect, the observations on the game by caricaturists and cartoonists often reflect this state of flux, and the various events which have brought the game into the forefront of the news have often given rise to a wealth of artistic material. During the 1950s and 1960s political cartoonists such as David Low and Victor Weisz ('Vicky'), neither of whom was a cricket enthusiast, often used the game to make a political point or analogy, and this has continued ever since.

In the work of two men in particular, Gerald Scarfe and Ralph Steadman, British caricature and cartoon have witnessed a fierceness of satire, an uncompromising note of social and political comment, and exaggeration and grotesqueness rarely seen since the days of Gillray. In 1977 Ralph Steadman travelled to Australia to witness the Centenary Test between Australia and England. A number of the cartoons he produced have an air of violence which, if exaggerated, is evident in the modern game, and his style contains something which had not previously been applied to cricket.

All is not gloom, however, and although startling, Steadman's cartoons are full of humour. And despite the rough waters through which it has had to sail, cricket is by no means off course or in danger of foundering. It still produces the great players and moments for newspaper cartoonists to depict, while at less exalted levels, in many ways it continues to be the game that has been played for decades. Indeed, whatever direction the game may take in the future, it is inconceivable that it will lose completely the huge spectrum of humour, ranging from the subtlest wit to outright hilarity, which it has built up over more than two centuries.

DENNIS LILLEE
Ralph Steadman (1936–)
1977. *The Listener*

Steadman was particularly struck by the manner in which Australian crowds relished the fast bowling of Dennis Lillee, who was the central figure of many of the cartoons. In this nightmarish scene the huge, monster-like figure of Lillee is shown bearing down upon a poor batsman – exactly as his fans most liked to see.

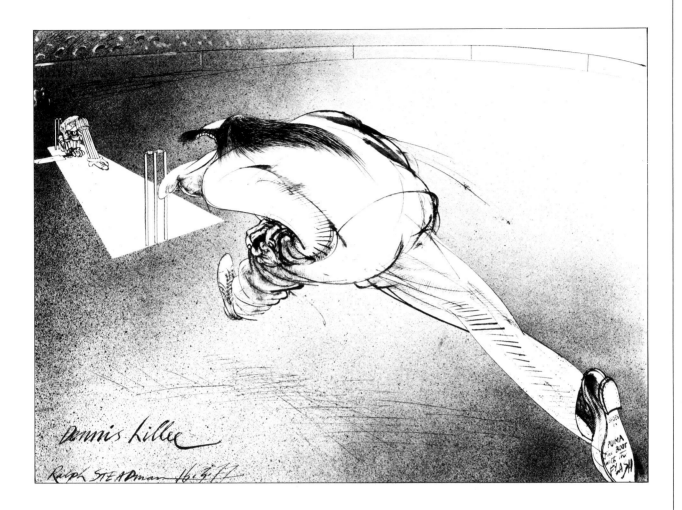

CHAPTER TWO

Cricket and Politics

The connection between cricket and politics has been important in the development of humorous cricket art, not least because political cartoons with cricket as the setting provide most of the early examples of the game's appearance in the genre. Certainly this is the case with the few examples which have survived from the eighteenth century. By the early decades of the nineteenth century, as cricket became slowly more established and more widely known, there developed a definite style which continued until the advent of *Punch* and cricket's rapid advance during the middle decades of the century. Given the subsequent richness of humorous illustration of the game these cartoons do not strike today's eye as being the most amusing or vividly drawn. None the less they are important, both as reflections of their own periods and because they established the link between the game and political caricature and cartoon which has remained strong ever since.

In 1760 a coloured print entitled 'The Cricket Players of Europe' (*see page 49*) was published depicting the various European heads of state playing cricket. Although the attribution of the print is not certain and one could not say definitely that it was the first time cricket had been used to illustrate a political situation, the cartoon is an important early example of this link between cricket and politics. It is interesting that the cartoon depicts international politics rather than English domestic affairs, although the fact that the scene is viewed through English eyes is made clear by the two figures in the foreground on the far right who are given the flattering captions of 'strength of will' and 'honour and courage'. The main protagonists are the batsman, Frederick the Great of Prussia, and the bowler, the Empress Maria Theresa of Austria.

WELLINGTON AND NAPOLEON
Attr: Thomas Landseer
(1795–1880)
c. 1815

Landseer's etching is a strange peculiarity among cricket cartoons and caricatures. The duke is defending his wicket, represented by the Three Graces, who carry a banner over their heads as the bail with the words 'A Bas le Tyrant'. Napoleon is the ball, shown with feet like those of a French cockerel. The duke's favoured status is confirmed by the owl of wisdom perched on his head.

Frederick and Maria Theresa were constantly at odds during the middle years of the eighteenth century, and the Prussian King is shown defending his wicket made of laurel leaves with his crown on top in the place of the bails. One of their many bones of contention was the state of Poland which is shown as a figure, seated and dejected in the foreground, with the caption of 'folly'. The three fielders are Russia (depicted as a woman, no doubt to represent the Empress Elizabeth), France (Louis XV), in front of whom lies a bat with the words 'treachery and infidelity' written upon it, and Turkey. The two umpires standing together are Holland, whose caption is 'cunning', and Spain – 'deceit'. All of the captions correspond to prevalent English opinions of the various countries at the time. Although the primary reason for the cartoon is political commentary, it is intriguing that the artist has made it a complete cricket scene by providing two scorers seated in the foreground, cutting notches for runs into their sticks in what was the customary manner until the early nineteenth century.

As one would expect from that time, 'The Cricket Players of Europe' is a rudimentary portrayal of the game of cricket, as is an etching done during the early years of the nineteenth century showing the great English hero of the time, the Duke

of Wellington, pitted against the great enemy Napoleon. The attribution is to Charles Landseer, elder brother of the famous Sir Edwin, but the date and style make it far more likely that the artist was Thomas, the eldest of the three Landseer brothers, in addition to which the monogram in the bottom left corner looks most like TL.

Thomas worked as a pupil and assistant to their father, John, an engraver, and it is known that in his earliest working years – when this must have been done as he was born in 1795 – he delighted in humorous engravings. His skill as an engraver continued to be the outstanding characteristic of his work throughout his career and he is best known for his engravings of his more illustrious brother's paintings, although one commentator supported him to the extent of maintaining that he evinced 'more originality and vigour of drawing than is to be seen in the excellently painted pictures of the more famous Sir Edwin'.

Stylistically Landseer's etching – if it is his – is certainly an oddity, but in its support of Wellington it represented the universal feeling in England at the time. Within a few years of the end of the Napoleonic Wars and the Duke's transition from soldiering to politics, the situation was rather different and critics of his unswerving Toryism were widespread.

The most prolific caricaturist of the 1830s and 1840s was John Doyle who confirmed the transition from Gillray, Rowlandson and Cruikshank to something far milder – and perhaps duller. It was commented on by W. M. Thackeray, himself a talented caricaturist during the 1830s before concentrating on his writing, in a manner which is most revealing both about Doyle and about the early Victorian public he was catering for. 'You never hear any laughing at HB; his pictures are a deal too genteel for that – polite points of wit, which strike one as exceedingly clever and pretty and cause one to smile in a quiet gentlemanlike kind of way.' Clever, pretty, smiling rather than laughing, gentlemanlike – all to become sought-after qualities in Victorian England.

The change was further emphasized by Doyle's use of a lithographic pencil which produced far softer lines than the deeper and harsher etchings of his predecessors. As is so often the case with cartoon and caricature, the style and humour of one generation are not those of another. Today Doyle's work does not have either great artistic impact or humorous appeal, but it is important to see it in the context

STATE CRICKET MATCH
John Doyle 'H.B.' (1797–1868)
1834. *Political Sketches No. 357*

of his time when it was both popular and influential.

John Doyle came to London from his native Ireland in 1822 and turned to political caricature in 1827 after an unsuccessful attempt to establish himself as a portrait painter. In 1829 he began the series of Political Sketches for which he became best known and which he was to continue until 1849, producing a total of some 1000 prints.

'State Cricket Match' was published by Maclean of Haymarket. Doyle supported Wellington, shown here bowling out the Whig Chancellor, Lord Brougham who is wielding his mace. Wellington is assisted by two fielders, King William IV and John Bull who cries 'Regularly bowled out by George'.

His influence can be seen in the technique of one of his contemporaries, Henry Heath, who used the monogram HH. Heath's imitation of Doyle's work is apparent in his cartoon 'A Cricket Match for a Sovereign', published as one of a series of political sketches in 1839. Here the target is Robert Peel, who is hit in the eye with the ball. The picture illustrates the rather complicated political situation at the time: Peel had established himself as the leader of a new Conservative Party which was at odds with the old Tories, such as the Duke of Wellington, who is the bowler. The presence of the young Queen Victoria as the central figure among the spectators suggests that the cartoon refers to events of 1839 when Peel was asked to form a government, but declined when the Queen refused to make changes in her household which he had requested. Behind the wicket is the Whig Lord John Russell, who later became a supporter of Peel, but at the time is sharing the joke with his neighbour whose comment, 'He has caught a peeler, Johnny', is the picture's caption.

If John Doyle's work represented the period of transition which took place during the 1830s and 1840s, his name was carried into the new era of *Punch* by his son Richard ('Dickie') who became with John Leech one of the magazine's first leading artists. Dickie Doyle, the father of Sir Arthur Conan Doyle, was a more versatile artist than his father, but he was reserved and a devout Catholic and, in 1850, a row with the

A CRICKET MATCH FOR A
SOVEREIGN
Henry Heath
1839

He has caught a *Peeler*, Johnny.

still youthful *Punch* over the magazine's anti-Catholic views led to his departure.

Around the time of Doyle's departure *Punch*'s editor, Mark Lemon, had noticed the work of John Tenniel whom he took on in 1850 and who was soon to eclipse both Leech and Doyle and, after Leech's death in 1864, to assume an unrivalled supremacy on the magazine which lasted until his retirement in 1901. Tenniel's career and influence were central to the development and establishment of *Punch*'s character and the Victorian humour it appealed to and represented. During the 1850s his drawings, which were engraved into woodblocks for the full-page political cartoons, set the magazine's style which lasted for half a century, and if not exactly copied by other *Punch* artists, his style was closely echoed.

Tenniel finally banished any waspish venom or hint of vulgarity from political cartoon, replacing them with illustrations of stately, sonorous humour. As one commentator concluded, 'Tenniel drew during his half-century of association with the paper over 2000 cartoons. They represented not only the essence of Victorian *Punch*, but of Victorian society, imperial, dignified and Olympian.' Curiously enough, Tenniel is more generally known to posterity for his original illustrations to Lewis Carroll's classics *Alice in Wonderland* and *Through the Looking-Glass* than for his work for *Punch*, and many critics, Bevis Hillier for one, consider that while his Alice creatures are unforgettable images which have never subsequently been bettered, his *Punch* cartoons did not achieve comparable life or impact.

One of Tenniel's foremost protégés on *Punch*, and the man who succeeded him as the magazine's first artist in 1901, was Edward Linley Sambourne. Sambourne was the great-grandfather of Princess Margaret's husband, the Earl of Snowdon, and gave his name to the title of their son, Lord Linley. He began drawing for *Punch* during the 1860s and to a large extent emulated the work of his senior, Tenniel, like whom he received a knighthood, in 1908.

Tenniel's influence is shown in Sambourne's picture of Gladstone and two lady cricketers which reveals how cricket was continuing to provide an ideal setting for making a political point – so long as it was done in the suitably proper and weighty *Punch* style. The picture, commenting on Gladstone's attitude to the growing movement for women's suffrage, appeared as a full-page political cartoon.

Sambourne's work suggests that the wood-blocks which were used for the *Punch* cartoons were partly responsible for the somewhat heavy lifelessness of many of the drawings. Certainly in his case, this at times disguised the great quality and vitality of his draughtsmanship evident in his original drawings, such as the one reproduced in Chapter Four.

Largely through the work of Bernard Partridge, who succeeded Sambourne as *Punch*'s artist on the latter's death in 1910, and that of Leonard Raven Hill, his accompanying second artist, the magazine's main political cartoons retained the basic style established by Tenniel until Partridge's death in 1945. By the turn of the century, however, the magazine's supremacy as the supplier of the best-known political cartoons was being challenged by the daily newspapers, who

THE POLITICAL LADY
CRICKETERS
Linley Sambourne (1845–1910)
1892. *Punch*

Lady Cricketer: 'A team of our own, I should think so! If we're good enough to scout for you why shouldn't we take a turn at the bat?'

were also producing the first truly sporting cartoons, such as those of 'Rip' (Roland Hill) and later Tom Webster.

The inter-war years saw the zenith of the popular dailies, owned and ruled by great magnates and – as yet unchallenged by radio or television – read by millions. Cartoons were an important part of their content and of all the cartoonists the one who established the greatest reputation was David Low, who was later knighted. Low, a New Zealander of Scots/Irish extraction, came to England after the First World War and joined the *Star*. It was during his twenty-three years with the *Evening Standard*, however, which he joined in 1927, that he achieved the height of his fame, in particular for his attacks on Hitler's Germany and a series of wartime cartoons.

UNITED NATIONS CLUB
David Low (1891–1963)
1945. *Evening Standard*

As this cartoon shows, Low drew with heavy strokes to produce strong outlines, in order that his work should retain its impact in the face of newspaper printing techniques and the medium of newsprint.

THE REMAINS OF THE
COMMONWEALTH
'Well, we've won The Ashes.'
Victor Weisz. 'Vicky'. (1913–66)
1962. *New Statesman*

Although Low was not himself a cricketing enthusiast, cricket and cricketers appear fairly regularly in his political cartoons. Slightly different from most, but one of the most apposite, is the cartoon he produced in June 1945 entitled 'United Nations Club'. The cartoon shows the four leaders of the Allies – Stalin, Churchill, Truman and de Gaulle – attired in the clothing and kit of their national sports. It is a typical Low touch that in the foreground is the somewhat bemused figure of a small boy who is voicing understandable scepticism about the club's potential for success.

It was inevitable that Churchill would be represented as a cricketer, and the cartoon confirms the extent to which cricket had become – and has remained – part of England's national identity. Just to look at his bat bearing the words 'British game' conjures up the idea of sportsmanship and the other qualities which have been equally important to the game and the nation. And of course, it is this very identification of the nation's attitudes with the game of cricket that has partly accounted for the wealth of cartoon material involving the sport.

Considering his New Zealand origins, one might not have expected David Low to put his finger so closely on to the pulse of English political life. Perhaps even more surprising was the success of Victor Weisz ('Vicky'), a Hungarian Jew who was born in Berlin and who left only to escape rising Nazism, coming to England in 1935. Low was both friend and mentor to Vicky, who shared his left-wing political views – if anything with a more radical edge.

Joining the *News Chronicle* during the late 1930s, Vicky worked there for nearly twenty years, eventually moving to the *Daily Mirror* and subsequently to the *Evening Standard*, where he succeeded Low. Throughout his career Vicky also worked for the *New Statesman*, and in 1962 he portrayed the Prime Minister, Harold Macmillan, uncomfortably trying to make the best of the break-up of Britain's colonies.

Vicky had produced his most famous image with his creation of 'Supermac' during the halcyon days of Macmillan's premiership, but here, with the horizons less rosy and only a year to go before the advent of the illness which forced his

NO APARTHEID
'That's not cricket.'
Vicky
1960. *New Statesman*

resignation, Macmillan looks anything but full of zest. On the wall behind one can just make out the bearded face and ample frame of W. G. Grace. In that cricket was such an important ingredient of England's relations with many of her colonies, and certainly the strongest sporting link between the various countries, the cartoon is entirely apt; however, as Vicky was not a cricket enthusiast, one irony of the scene had possibly escaped him, which is the fact that at the time England did not even hold the Ashes, Richie Benaud's team having retained them for Australia during the summer of 1961.

In contrast to cases where cricket has been used to provide the setting for political cartoon is the one post-war political issue which cricket itself initiated and which has had a long-running and acrimonious effect upon the game – as it has upon a great many other sports: South Africa and the apartheid question. Here is a case where international politics reared its ugly head in an unprecedented manner and cricket was – however much against its will – inexorably involved. Even the most serious previous international cricket crisis, over the Bodyline question during England's tour of Australia in 1932–3, was essentially a cricketing question which reached political levels only during a brief period of extreme tension.

The political direction that South Africa was taking became evident some years before apartheid was to affect cricket so directly and disastrously. It was certainly clear to Vicky who, as a socialist with strong liberal and humanitarian ideals, found apartheid totally abhorrent. In a brutally vivid cartoon drawn in April 1960, captioned 'That's not cricket', he illustrated how the South African regime would inevitably cast its shadow over sport.

It was not until 1968 that the issue provoked a cricketing crisis. The flashpoint was the announcement by the South African Premier, Mr Vorster, that the Cape coloured player, Basil d'Oliveira, would not be an acceptable member of the England team due to tour South Africa under the MCC flag in the winter of 1968–9. Initially England had not selected d'Oliveira for the tour, despite his strong qualifications, thus giving the impression that they were bowing to pressure from South Africa, and he had been selected only after another player became unavailable.

As a result of South Africa's unacceptable demands, the MCC called off the tour. A little over a year later South Africa

ANTI-APARTHEID
DEMONSTRATOR
Raymond Jackson. 'Jak'
1970. *Evening Standard*

On a number of occasions the MCC members, invariably drawn by Jak with military moustaches, blazers and wearing the club's striped tie, have provided rich material for his humour.

were due to make a return visit to England. During the winter of 1969–70, however, their rugby team, the Springboks, had toured England and been greeted with scenes of constant disturbance and violence as anti-apartheid protestors demonstrated unceasingly. Although the MCC hung on as long as possible in the hope that the cricket tour could go ahead, at the eleventh hour they bowed to pressure from the Government and called off the tour.

In a cartoon which appeared in 1970 with a far more light-hearted tone than Vicky's earlier one, Jak of the *Evening Standard* illustrates the possibility of disturbance by anti-apartheid demonstrators, and in doing so makes fun of both the average anti-apartheid protestor and the seemingly all-powerful figures of the MCC.

Apartheid has been the longest-lasting and most damaging political question to have affected cricket since the war, but it has been by no means the only one and, in general terms, the modern game – greatly more international than it ever was before – has become increasingly political. Many observers feel that the established ethics of the game as first and foremost a sport are under permanent threat from a host of

political enemies, be it the internal politics of running the game in England or strained relations between two Test-playing countries.

At the level of international relations, nowhere have they been more strained in Test cricket than between the neighbouring countries of India and Pakistan. During the autumn of 1987 the two countries jointly hosted the fourth World Cup competition of one-day internationals and the potential for rivalry and disagreement seemed limitless. In a cartoon for *Punch*, John Jensen makes the cheering point that cricket can often be a pacifying and unifying influence (*see page 56*). On either side of their border Pakistani and Indian soldiers, both wearing tee-shirts with the message 'cricket for peace', enjoy the same commentary from a match in Peshawar, temporarily relaxing and shouldering their guns. In addition, the cartoon has a little cameo of Allan Border, captain of the Australian side, who eventually secured a surprise victory in the competition.

In recent years Jensen has been *Punch*'s leading sporting artist, providing pictures full of life and humour, and often delightful exaggeration. It is a credit to the magazine that, nearly 150 years after its foundation, it still occupies a central position in British caricature and cartoon.

CHAPTER THREE

Some Portraits

For most people it is the personalities of cricket who have always provided the greatest interest and enjoyment. Many have assumed enormous reputations, become heroes and household names, and presented ideal material for caricaturists and cartoonists. A select number of these caricatures are, without doubt, among the highlights of cricketing art.

During the early decades of the game's development caricatures of the players were rare, partly because cricket had not yet come to sufficient prominence and partly because 'portrait-charge' caricatures were neither a fashionable nor a popular medium. But as we have seen, things changed steadily during the Victorian era, as sport and sportsmen became a more important part of the fabric of English life and, in 1868, the launch of *Vanity Fair* by Thomas Gibson Bowles provided a magazine which was to become best known for its elegant, witty and normally polite caricatures.

Cricketers were only occasionally the subject of the magazine's famous weekly caricatures, for, as John Arlott explains, 'Selection as the subject of the *Vanity Fair* cartoon conferred a stamp of importance – sufficient importance to be publicly praised or attacked – and, since the choice was taken from all fields of activity and from all countries, cricketers were not portrayed very frequently.' None the less, between the magazine's initiation and 1913, the last year that it appeared under its original name, around forty cricketers and cricketing personalities appeared in various guises. No cricketer was selected for the nine years after *Vanity Fair*'s foundation until 1877, when W. G. Grace appeared, drawn by Spy. Anyone surprised that he had not appeared earlier should remember that at this time Grace was not yet thirty and his years of real triumph and fame were to come, in the 1880s and 1890s.

Vanity Fair's first caricaturist was the Italian Carlo Pellegrini, or Ape, whose work was decisive in the magazine's

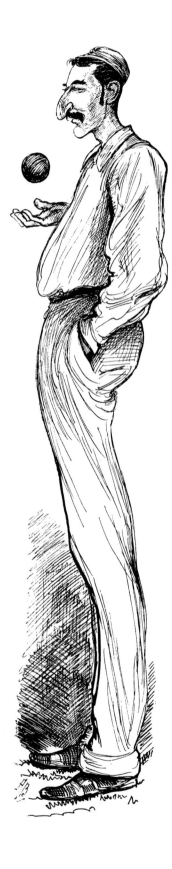

F. R. SPOFFORTH (1853–1926)
'A.B.'
1884. *World*

Despite the uncertainty of the artist's identity this pen and ink study of 'The Demon' Spofforth, which appeared as one of a pair with a study of W. G. Grace, is a caricature of quality and humour. The fact that Spofforth appeared with 'The Champion' clearly shows the reputation he achieved. Exaggerating by its thinness Spofforth's formidable height of 6ft 2ins, it captures perfectly the Australian as he appeared to the English public; confident, relaxed and humorously relishing the task of dismissing their batsmen.

rapid success. He set the style with his first caricature, of the Prime Minister Benjamin Disraeli, a commission that was not all plain sailing. According to another cartoonist, Harry Furniss, when Ape enquired of Disraeli's secretary about the possibility of a sitting with the great statesman, the answer was, 'Can't be done Carlo . . . but I'll trot him out of doors for you tomorrow and walk him up and down until you have made your sketch and he will be none the wiser.'

Ape's portrait of George Bonnor (*see page 51*) is far more agreeable than that of his other cricketer, the Hon. Alfred Lyttelton, and the pose captures instantly the Australian's great stature, confirmed in part of the accompanying description: 'He is a quiet, amiable, low-voiced, comely giant, standing six feet six in his boots, measuring forty-five inches round the chest, and weighing seventeen stone all but two pounds.'

Bonnor visited England with Australian teams five times, in 1880, 1882, 1884, 1886 and 1888, and although he never achieved outstanding scores he captured the public's imagination with his enormous hitting, which seemed to complement his vast frame. He was affectionately referred to as the 'Colonial Hercules' and it was generally agreed that he was the only batsman whose hitting rivalled the greatest English hitter at that time – or probably at any time – C. I. Thornton. In the first Test in England, at The Oval in 1880, with the stroke that ended his innings Bonnor hit the ball so high that the batsmen were on their third run before it came down – into the trembling hands of Fred Grace, who died two weeks after the match.

It must have been a measure of Bonnor's personality that he was chosen to appear as 'Australian Cricket' in *Vanity Fair* shortly after the end of the three-match Test series of 1884 rather than, for instance, the Australian captain, Murdoch, who in the last match at The Oval scored the first Test double-century.

A few weeks after Ape's caricature of Bonnor appeared in *Vanity Fair*, in November 1884, another member of the Australian Test side, F. R. Spofforth, was drawn in the publication *World*, by an artist with the monogram AB. Spofforth had already appeared in *Vanity Fair* and 'The Demon', as he was universally known, was the most renowned Australian cricketer of the nineteenth century. His fast bowling was admired and feared, and from the time of the match at Lord's in 1878 between the Australians and the MCC, when he took six for 4 in the first innings and five for 16 in the second, he regularly produced fearsome, match-winning performances.

Ape's understudy at *Vanity Fair* during the early years was the caricaturist whose name was to become most synonymous with the magazine – Spy, or Sir Leslie Ward. During the forty-odd years of Vanity Fair's life Spy contributed 1000 of the total of nearly 2500 cartoons which appeared. He was knighted in 1918. His caricatures were far gentler than Ape's and were often close to straight portraiture of a flattering, elegant, but at times rather uninteresting type. Nevertheless he was hugely popular in late Victorian and Edwardian England and his quantities of caricatures for *Vanity Fair* have been constantly reprinted ever since.

Among the many cricketers whom he portrayed were the game's two premier peers, Lords Harris and Hawke, who were both to play a crucial role for the MCC as the club's Treasurer – a post which they held successively. It is therefore entirely fitting that the club is fortunate enough to possess Spy's original pen and watercolour sketches of the two carica-tures, as well as one of R. A. H. Mitchell (*see page 50*). For many years Mitchell ran the cricket at Eton and Lords Harris and Hawke were two of his more distinguished products. It is only in these original pictures, as compared with any subse-quent prints made of them, that one gets a real impression of the skill and humour behind Spy's deft lines and colouring.

Lord Harris was the second English cricketer after Grace to appear in *Vanity Fair*, and rightly so (*see page 51*). Grace was the premier player and cricketing figure in the public eye, but Harris was the game's foremost pillar of authority. The caption of Spy's caricature is 'Kent', Lord Harris's home county for which he played for forty years and captained for nearly twenty, laying the foundations for the county's great years at the beginning of this century, when they won the Championship in 1906, 1909, 1910 and 1913.

Few people dared to question his lordship's authority, but he was universally respected because his autocratic tendencies were always balanced by absolute fairness. His attacks on players, for instance during the throwing crisis of the 1880s, were prompted by a determination that the game should be played honestly and strictly by the laws.

Above
REGENCY CRICKET
Henry Heath
(career 1824–50)

Below
THE CRICKET PLAYERS
OF EUROPE
Artist Unknown
1760

A coloured print showing the various European rulers involved in a game of cricket and possibly the first example of cricket being used to portray a political situation.

Left
R. A. H. MITCHELL (1843–1905)
'Mike'
Sir Leslie Ward. 'Spy'. (1851–1922)
1896. *Vanity Fair*

Spy's portrait of R. A. H. Mitchell was one of his most charming and sympathetic studies for *Vanity Fair*. His subject was aged over fifty and the artist, with the combination of the stance, the tilt of the boater and the slight smile, managed to capture all the benignity and Edwardian elegance of this senior gentleman.

R. A. H. Mitchell was a brilliant young amateur cricketer, a blue all his four years at Oxford (1862–65), and generally considered the outstanding batsman to have been to either university. He never went on to play county or Test cricket, returning in 1866 to Eton, where he had been at school, to become an assistant master. For the next thirty years he devoted himself to Eton cricket and one has only to glance at a list of the amateur batsmen of the Golden Age to see how impressive was his list of products.

Right
LORD HARRIS (1851–1933)
'Kent'
Spy
1881. *Vanity Fair*

By the time Spy's caricature of Lord Harris appeared in *Vanity Fair* Harris had been captain of Kent for over a decade and had, in the previous year, captained England in the historic First Test against Australia at The Oval.

Far right
GEORGE BONNOR (1855–1912)
Carlo Pellegrini. 'Ape'. (1838–89)
1884. *Vanity Fair*

Ape only drew two cricketers for *Vanity Fair*, of whom George Bonnor was the first.

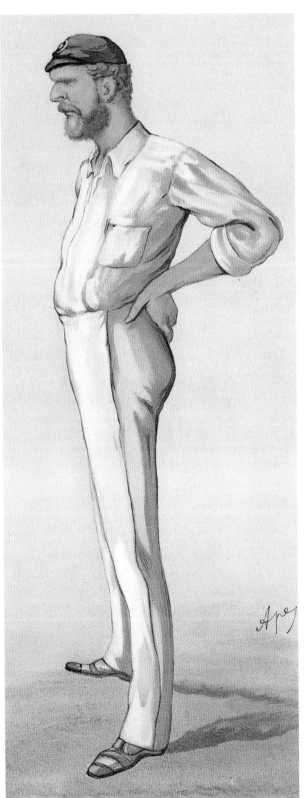

Left
RODNEY MARSH (1947–)
Ralph Steadman
1977. *The Listener*

Below
JOHN ARLOTT
'Never caught'
Ralph Steadman
1977. *The Listener*

Left
LORD HAWKE (1860–1938)
'Yorkshire'
Spy
1892. *Vanity Fair*

Although he was only thirty-two when the picture appeared Lord Hawke was in his tenth season as captain of Yorkshire whose fortunes he had transformed. Surprisingly, perhaps, Hawke wears the cap and blazer of the I Zingari, the famous wandering club whose closest links have always been with Lord Harris's county, Kent.

GROTESQUE BORDERS
George Woodward
1799

Above left
CRICKET MATCH
EXTRAORDINARY
A grand female match between 11 of
Surrey and 11 of Hampshire
Thomas Rowlandson
1811

GREENWICH v CHELSEA
HOSPITAL PENSIONERS
MATCH
Henry Alken snr (1785–1851)
c. 1825

Right

The back of the picture carries the caption: 'Yesterday morning the eleven men with one arm, and eleven men with one leg, were brought by three Greenwich stages engaged for that purpose to the new cricket ground, at the back of Montpelier Tea Gardens, Walworth, when the match was played out and the ones with one leg beat the one arms by 103 runnings.

'After the match was finished the eleven one-legged men ran a sweep-stake, of one hundred yards distance for 20 guineas, and the first three had prizes.'

ONE-ARM AND
ONE-LEG MATCH
Henry (H.G.) Alken jnr

56

Left
WORLD CUP 1987
John Jensen (1930–)
1987. *Punch*

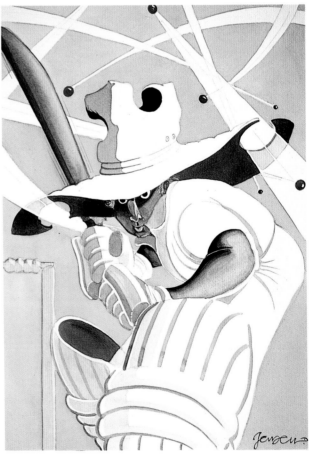

Right
SUNIL GAVASKAR (1949–)
John Jensen
1987. *Punch*

As Lord Harris was establishing his regime in Kent, at the other end of the country, in Yorkshire, Lord Hawke, who Spy drew for *Vanity Fair* in 1892, was exerting similar authority to the benefit of his county. Captain of Yorkshire from 1881 until 1910 and President from 1898 until his death in 1938, Lord Hawke ruled his professionals, dismissing those with a liking for drink – from which many professionals suffered at the time – while conscientiously looking after their interests by introducing winter pay. His efforts brought spectacular results and Yorkshire were champion county eight times during his captaincy. As well as his rule over Yorkshire, Lord Hawke played an important role in the spread of cricket by taking a number of tours overseas.

Spy may have been the most prolific of *Vanity Fair*'s artists, but the man who is almost invariably considered to have been the most brilliant and witty caricaturist to have contributed to the magazine was Max Beerbohm. Although he certainly influenced future artists, Max's style as a caricaturist was quite unique. Also it brought a welcome return of some of the qualities of caricature which had virtually disappeared since the great days of the late eighteenth century: outrageous exaggeration, waspish humour and satire, as well as the foremost of Max's own talents – the ability to mock in the most elegant manner imaginable. His style is summed up in his own definition of caricature: 'The most perfect caricature is that which, on a small surface, with the simplest means, most accurately exaggerates to the highest point the peculiarities of a human being, at his most characteristic moment, in the most beautiful manner.'

Max's pen and ink caricature of W. G. Grace hangs in the Pavilion at Lord's and one feels that it was a happy stroke of fortune which led to the 'champion' being drawn by such a master, especially considering that he only ever drew one other cricketer, Ranji.

The great majority of Max's caricatures were of actors, artists and writers from the London of the 1890s which he himself knew so intimately. Like all devoted and skilful social observers, though, he was constantly being amused and tempted by different possible subjects, and in 1895 he found an ideal one in W. G. Grace. The thought of playing cricket or any sport would have appalled Max, but he would have been fascinated by the stature W.G. had gained and been captivated by his appearance.

Left
W. G. GRACE (1848–1915)
Max Beerbohm (1872–1956)
1895

'Portrait of dear old W.G. – to the left is the Grand Stand; to the right the funeral of one of his patients.'

1895 was Grace's glorious Indian summer when he defied both his age and all expectations. Approaching his forty-seventh birthday, he opened the season with a century and one week later became the first man to score 100 centuries with an innings of 288 against Somerset. A fortnight later he became the first batsman to score 1000 runs in May. He finished the season with 2346 runs, easily the highest aggregate of any batsman that year.

Right
A CENTURY OF GRACE
Harry Furniss (1854–1925)
1895. *New Budget*

Furniss was primarily a *Punch* artist who worked for the magazine from 1873 until 1894. A rumbustious Irishman, he could also be highly cantankerous – no doubt the reason that he was never on the salaried staff of *Punch* and certainly the reason for his sudden departure after a row in 1894.

It would seem an impossible task, using only pen and ink sketches, with no other figure or background involved, to sustain both interest and humour through one hundred pictures of the same man in the same attire doing essentially the same thing. Furniss accomplished it with extraordinary ease.

PATTING THE CREASE   HIS FIRST OVER   NOT YET!   TAKING IT EASY   CAREFUL

CUTTING   A RUN FOR FOUR   BLOWN

WARM WORK

IS IT A RUN?   GINGERLY   NOT FOR W. G.!   A CRACK   A BLOW

IN FULL BLAST

Grace fills the centre of the drawing with his enormous frame and forearms, and dense mass of beard. He holds in one hand a ridiculously small bat while in the other is a cheque for £10,000, signed 'Edward Lawson'. This was the total raised by a 'shilling fund' set up by the *Daily Telegraph*, of which Sir Edward Lawson was the proprietor, to mark Grace's hundred centuries. Max himself contributed a shilling to the fund, but, as he made clear, 'not in support of cricket but as an earnest protest against golf'.

The Lord's Pavilion also contains a selection from a series of sketches of Grace done by Harry Furniss in 1895 which, with Max's picture, was a marvellous year for cricket caricature. Again to mark the hundred centuries, Furniss produced a series of one hundred sketches of W.G. entitled 'A Century of Grace', which first appeared in the *New Budget*.

The sketches were arranged to provide a running commentary on his performances with bat, ball and in the field: prodding forward, hitting out, starting a run . . . sending his partner back, taking a rest, mopping his brow, bowling round-arm, or bending for a catch. Each was accompanied by a short caption to complete the humour and some of them are funny on their own: 'Fielding, a Study in Backs', 'Is it a Run . . . Gingerly . . . Not for W.G.!', 'The Champion Bowls but not the Champion Bowler', and 'The Final Bow'.

If Grace was without question the most regularly portrayed and caricatured cricketer towards the end of the nineteenth century, another with enormous appeal, whose Test career was just starting, was the Indian prince Ranjitsinhji. Ranji played in his first Test in 1896, three years before Grace's last. Oriental princes intrigued nineteenth-century Englishmen – and here was one who not only outdid most English gentlemen with his sartorial elegance and modest courtesy, but who also played cricket for England. His batting was one of the great joys of the turn of the century years.

One cartoonist for whom Ranji held endless appeal was Rip, who drew him in an endless variety of guises: some highly imaginative, such as the 'Ranjipanther' which he created, others more pure caricature, such as the series in his *Kricket Karicatures* of 1896. Here Ranji is shown in various poses, always willowy and impeccable whether batting, fielding or in a suit and boater carrying his bag.

Another of Rip's favourite characters was Sammy Woods, the Somerset player who was one of the best-loved cricketers

RANJITSINHJI (1872–1933)
Rip
1896. *Kricket Karicatures*

Left
SAMMY (S.M.J.) Woods
(1867–1931)
Rip
1907
_____

Rip's composite caricature of Woods is in a style he often used, showing a player in a series of typical poses. No doubt he was thinking of Sammy's home ground of Taunton with the caption of 'Into the River', for the River Tone flows along one side of the ground. The other batting pose of Woods playing doggo captioned 'Can Play the Goose game' was seen less frequently. Of the other sketches, 'Fond of the White Rose' is a humorous reference to Somerset's giant-killing rate of success against the all-powerful Yorkshire when they (Somerset) were still a very junior competitor in the County Championship. From 1900–03 Yorkshire were champions all three years and lost only two matches – both to Somerset, who beat them again in 1904.

Right
P. G. H. FENDER (1892–1985)
Tom Webster
1924. *Daily Mail*
_____

At the time of this cartoon, Yorkshire were enjoying another period of seeming invincibility; champions from 1922–25, during which time they lost just six matches. Their strength as well as the general unsuitability of the comparison only increased the humour of Webster's regular portrayal of the county as a diminutive terrier. The depth of their batting accounts for the terrier's lack of a tail.

during the last years of the nineteenth century and early years of the twentieth. Born in Australia, Woods came to England aged seventeen and, after giving an inkling of his cricketing potential at school, went up to Cambridge where he was a Blue for all four years he was there. It was at Cambridge that his prowess as a fast bowler was made evident and in the four matches against Oxford, of which Cambridge won three with the fourth drawn, Woods took a total of 36 wickets.

His fast bowling was later put to good effect for the Gentlemen against the Players, notably in 1894 when F. S. Jackson and he bowled unchanged through both innings. But it was in Somerset, the county for which he played from 1886 until 1910, that he gave the most enjoyment and where he is still so affectionately remembered. One feels he must have been an irresistible personality; a huge man – but wonderfully built – with a thick mass of hair so that W.G. called him 'shock 'ead', he was usually laughing, enjoyed every moment of life and was as generous as he was humorous. As a cricketer he was the crowd's ideal combination, a fast bowler and big hitter, his batting coming to the fore around the mid 1890s.

As a newspaper cartoonist Rip had plenty of opportunity to draw his favourite cricketers as often as he liked. The same was true for Tom Webster who, as well as his output of cartoons with a running commentary, produced some outstanding caricatures of his favourite players. One of these was P. G. H. Fender, whom Webster drew in 1924 with the huge spectacles, moustache, fuzzy hair and long sweater which he inevitably gave him.

At the time, Fender was captain of Surrey; many people considered that he should have been captain of England and only the fact that he was Jewish prevented him from being offered the post by the MCC. More important for Webster, he was one of the great characters of inter-war cricket: witty but combative, an exceptionally shrewd captain, outstanding in the slips and – most of all – a batsman who by his power and fast scoring became one of the great crowd-pullers of all time and, at Northampton in 1920, took the record for the fastest hundred ever, scored in 35 minutes.

When Fender played for England in 1921 there was in the opposing Australian team which won so decisively a leg-spin and googly bowler who has the distinction of being the only Test cricketer who was also a professional cartoonist – Arthur Mailey. Mailey's style of bowling and his wit complemented each other perfectly, and his humour usually carried a note of self-deprecation which is best exhibited in his autobiography *Ten for 66 and All That*, but which is also essential to the self-portrait caricature which he drew.

Mailey's quite individual, Australian brand of humour was in total contrast to the style of James Thorpe, a cricket-lover whose cartoons between the wars, for *Punch*, other magazines and for his book *A Cricket Bag*, were unmistakably English. The inspiration for the bulk of Thorpe's work is pointed to by a comment he made in the introduction to his biography of Phil May, a great *Punch* artist of the 1890s: 'The two heroes of my boyhood were W. G. Grace and Phil May, and they have never been altogether supplanted.'

The MCC is fortunate to possess a large collection of the original drawings of Thorpe's work, including a collection of series of various Test sides – English and visiting – produced for *Punch* during the 1930s. These portrait caricatures all bear the clearly recognizable signs of Thorpe's simple style, with elegant lines and the overall effect of light, inoffensive humour.

THE FAMOUS AUSTRALIAN 'GOOGLY' BOWLER
A. A. Mailey (1886–1967)
Self-portrait
1921

ABSENT FRIENDS
James Thorpe
1931. *Punch*
——————————

As one of his series of caricatures of
New Zealand's tour in 1931, executed
for *Punch*, Thorpe drew a group of five
England cricketers who had not played
in the First Test: Hobbs, Duckworth,
Tate, Chapman and Hendren.

MAURICE TATE (1895–1956)
James Thorpe
c. 1930

ENGLAND'S BULWARK
'Jardine went on doing this for hours
and hours and hours.'
James Thorpe
1932. *Punch*

Left
IN THE NETS
Headley and his new bat
James Thorpe
1933

On the first of his two visits to England,
George Headley arrived with a considerable reputation, not least thanks
to his success against the Australian
bowlers on their home grounds in
1930–31. Thorpe's caricature is a delightful cameo with just the hint of the
cavalier twinkle which people automati-
cally came to associate with Headley.

Below
THE MAHARAJ'S CATCH
James Thorpe
1936

A cricketer of somewhat less obvious
talent than George Headley was the
captain of the visiting Indians in 1936,
the Maharaj Kumar of Vizianagram.
Admittedly he did take one catch in the
First Test, but his tubby, bespectacled
figure was the source of far more
amusement than admiration for
English crowds.

The inter-war years saw a host of highly popular cricketers
who enthralled crowds and were worshipped by their supporters, but never was there a time quite like the years
immediately after the Second World War when English cricket-
lovers craved for players who, by a combination of skill and
personality, could remind them of the good side of life. One
batsman in particular, Denis Compton, fitted the bill ideally.
As John Warr wrote of him in *Barclays World of Cricket*:
'Cavalier in approach with a showman's flair and a genius for
the game, he poured out his skill to a captivated public.'

Compton's career with Middlesex and England began before the war, but it was during the summer of 1947 that he
reached record-breaking heights, scoring 3816 runs in the
season, including eighteen hundreds. Debonair, and with more
than a touch of the devil-may-care, Compton was as irresistible as the film stars the public packed into cinemas to watch.

A clear indication of his huge reputation was his inclusion in a book of caricatures by David Low, called *Low's
Company* and published in 1952. The book contains fifty

DENIS COMPTON (1918–)
David Low
1952

caricatures of leading personalities of the day and, among a distinguished selection of politicians, actors and artistic figures, Compton was the only sportsman. Drawn like all the others in thick charcoal, he is shown as his public liked him when he was not batting, smiling jauntily, with the famous 'Brylcreem' wave in his hair.

If Compton possessed some of the attractions of a film star, the comparison could not be less apt for another post-war cricketer who became one of the game's leading personalities – Alec Bedser. There was nothing glamorous about Bedser, but his tirelessness, which combined with his immense ability to make him England's outstanding bowler of the post-war years, his down-to-earth honesty and transparent devotion to cricket and its principles, made him universally popular, first as a player and later as a selector and administrator. With his identical twin brother Eric, who also played for Surrey, he made up a double act with endless potential for cartoonists.

On his own, Bedser is usually thought of as he is shown in a caricature by Roy Ullyett called 'The Big Fella'. Ullyett, a sporting cartoonist who worked for the *Daily Express* from 1953 and also drew for *Punch* for many years, continuing the magazine's high standard, shows Bedser on his home ground of The Oval – the gentle giant that he was, sleeves rolled up, huge hands almost enveloping the ball and his discarded jersey swamping the unfortunate figure of the diminutive umpire.

In 1962, just as it was announced that the distinction between gentlemen and players was being ended and when it seemed that the role of the gentleman amateur in cricket was on the decline, the MCC made the surprise decision of appointing the Duke of Norfolk as manager of the team to tour Australia during the coming winter. The Duke was a lifelong devotee of cricket, particularly as host at the private ground of his Sussex home, Arundel Castle, and had been President of the MCC in 1957. In the event, the Duke's management of the tour was an unqualified success but, not surprisingly, it caused a certain amount of amusement both in Australia and at home, as shown in Vicky's caricature of him which appeared in the *New Statesman* just before the Second Test of the tour, which England won.

There could be no greater contrast than between the be- nignly humorous portraits such as Ullyett's Bedser or Vicky's Duke of Norfolk, and the work of one of England's fiercest post-war cartoonists, Ralph Steadman. Best known for his

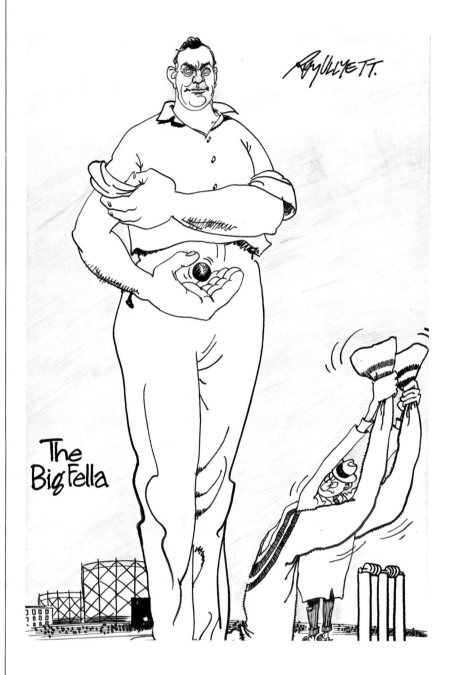

The Big Fella

ALEC BEDSER (1918–)
'The big fella'
Roy Ullyett (1914–)
c. 1950

prolific quantity of work on political or social subjects, Steadman made his mark on the game of cricket when, in 1977, he was asked to draw for *The Listener* a series of cartoons of the Centenary Test between England and Australia in Melbourne.

Steadman's cartoons show the game as anything but the gentle pastime of popular imagination, and would not suit the taste of many cricket enthusiasts. Like all cartoonists, however, Steadman's work has a strong streak of realism and the

THE DUKE OF NORFOLK
(1908–75)
Vicky
1962. *New Statesman*

It was a rare occasion that Vicky worked outside the sphere of pure politics for, as his close friend James Cameron once remarked, 'he was the most political human being I have ever met'. It was equally unusual for a duke to find his way onto the pages of the *New Statesman*.

violence which he highlights, with batsmen cowering at the crease and supporters baying for blood, is by no means totally imaginary. His portrait of Rodney Marsh (*see page 53*) shows the stocky Australian wicket-keeper grotesquely exaggerated as he crouches behind the stumps and yet, repugnant though it may be, the caricature is rich in humour and irony.

How different to this startling, blood-spattered Marsh portrait is Steadman's infinitely subtle caricature of John Arlott as a cricket ball (*see page 53*). For decades John Arlott's voice personified radio commentary of cricket – mellow, soporific, but always astute and full of humour.

Radio and, to a greater extent, television, have revolutionized the presentation of cricket and commentary on the game, mostly for the good but occasionally with detrimental results. Fortunately, however, television will never be able to supersede humorous illustration of the game, which is today as buoyant as ever. Inevitably the focus is upon the leading players as it always has been, and no player has been the subject of more attention – as often critical as congratulatory – as Ian Botham. Botham's achievements as an all-rounder speak for themselves and there is no denying that for a decade he has been the biggest crowd-puller in the game. All the same, his reputation has too often been sullied by his antics on and off the field. Many observers cannot decide whether – as his supporters would have it – underneath all his bravado he is just a bluff, big-hearted likeable chap.

John Jensen, who has studied and drawn Botham on countless occasions in recent years, is prepared to give him the benefit of the doubt in his caricature of Botham as he imagines him in retirement. Gone is all the razzmatazz and here is our Ian, telling a yarn: portly and red-cheeked in baggy trousers and wellies and even wearing a tie, although the strands of hair suggest that he might not have subsided totally into comfortable middle-age.

Jensen's cartoon appeared in August 1987, when it was announced that Botham would not be playing for England during the coming winter. Another England player who decided to opt out for a rest was David Gower, a man of markedly different personality. Indeed, as Jensen's two portraits highlight, Botham and Gower, at the same time as being the two leading characters in the England side of recent years – the one the swashbuckling all-rounder and big-hitter, the other the nonchalant stylist – have also

IAN BOTHAM (1955–)
DAVID GOWER (1957–)
John Jensen
1987. *Punch*

Jensen's speculative ideas as to how these two England players will turn out once they have retired from cricket.

represented two extremes of the modern first-class cricketer.

Another player who represents a different extreme is the Indian batsman Sunil Gavaskar, whom Jensen drew earlier in 1987 as Gavaskar became the first man in history to score 10,000 Test runs (*see page 56*). The quality of Jensen's caricature lies in the combination of its imagination and accuracy. Here is the little man as he so often appeared, crouching in front of the wicket under an enormous wide-brimmed hat, impervious to the volley of balls around him, his eyes waiting steadfastly for the one he can despatch to the boundary. In his amassing of runs in the never-ending round of Test cricket Gavaskar could be seen as the supreme example of the modern batsman — the only thing that detracts from this in Jensen's portrait is his floppy hat, today almost universally replaced by a safety helmet.

CHAPTER FOUR

The Field of Play

The most important single strand running through cricket caricature and cartoon is the humorous possibilities intrinsic in the action of the game – whoever the players and whatever the setting. There is a sameness about the way every footballer kicks his ball, or the way every golfer strikes his – at least to the inexpert eye – from which one could never accuse bowlers or batsmen of suffering. And when calamity occurs – the duck, the dropped catch, the series of long-hops carted to the boundary – it is plain for all to see and, to be honest, to enjoy while outwardly murmuring sympathetically.

It was the game's ridiculous possibilities – heightened admittedly on this occasion by the fact that the players were ladies – which attracted Thomas Rowlandson to produce a watercolour cartoon which is one of the most treasured pictures at Lord's. The cartoon is well known in colour and black and white copies but, as is so often the case, a certain vitality and immediacy is lost which can be enjoyed only in the original.

Like his contemporary James Gillray, Rowlandson was a master of political satire – not being afraid to lampoon the high and mighty and having no strong political allegiances himself. The difference between the two men was that in Gillray's case political satire dominated his output, but for Rowlandson it was only one string to his bow. Perhaps as a result of having a more relaxed outlook he was often happy as an amused observer, taking in scenes from English life. Rowlandson made a series of leisurely tours around the country which provided plenty of material for illustration, such as the series about his character Dr Syntax, the first of which appeared in 1812.

Many situations and 'types' appealed to Rowlandson, not least ample ladies in a state of disarray. His most famous cartoon on this theme was 'Exhibition Stare-Case', making fun of the annual Royal Academy exhibition and showing unfortunate ladies tumbling down the stairs of Somerset House, many in an advanced state of *déshabille*, within full view of – and in some cases within the grasp of – the gentlemen Academicians.

'Exhibition Stare Case' appeared in 1811 and it was similarly proportioned ladies who were the players in his picture of the same year entitled 'Rural Sports, or a Cricket Match Extraordinary' (*see page 54*). In fact, ladies' cricket had been well established since the late eighteenth century, but this was no reason for Rowlandson not to indulge his sense of humour. Like all his cartoons, the picture clearly reveals his wonderful draughtsmanship and a facility of line and colour wash which enabled him to work at great speed.

The match was reported in the *News*:

On Wednesday last a singular cricket match commenced at Ball's Pond, Newington. The players on each side [sic] were twenty-two women: eleven Hampshire against eleven Surrey. The Match was made between two noblemen of the respective counties for five hundred guineas aside.

The performers in this singular contest were of all ages and sizes, from 14 years old to upwards of 40; and the different parties were distinguished by coloured ribbons: Royal purple for the Hampshire; orange and blue, Surrey. The weather being favourable on Wednesday, some very excellent play, and much skill was displayed; but the palm of that day was borne off by a Hampshire lass who made a 41 innings before she was thrown out . . . the game, it is expected, will be concluded to-morrow; but the general opinion is that Hampshire will gain the victory.

The scene would have been irresistible to Rowlandson – the ladies with their full skirts tucked up above their knees to enable them to run, some falling about in the deep in their attempts to chase or catch the ball, inevitably exposing more than just their knees. As well as its rich humour the cartoon also gives a good idea of what the average cricketing scene would have looked like during the Regency period: two scorers sitting in the foreground still counting runs by cutting notches into a stick (although in major matches this would probably have been replaced with a scorebook by now), and on the far side a tent flying the 'Jolly Cricketers' flag, no doubt the place to lay a wager and providing for thirsty spectators. It is probable that the wicket would have been three stumps by this time, rather than the two shown by Rowlandson, but it is an insignificant detail in a picture of such quality.

In addition to his skills as an artist, Rowlandson was an expert engraver and in this capacity produced much work in partnership with a contemporary artist George Woodward. Woodward was particularly fond of satirizing appearances and social habits, rather than making fun of specific people or events. In 1796 he produced a series of sketches called 'Grotesque Borders', engraved by Rowlandson and including a cricket scene – a very early appearance of the game in a cartoon (*see page 54*). Some of the more bizarre groups of cricket cartoons are those depicting matches between players with either one arm or one leg – of which there is a surprisingly large number. One picture by Henry Alken, the original of which is at Lord's, is a gem of humorous art, however little one may find funny the spectacles of cripples hobbling around on wooden legs or waving wooden arms. The picture is called 'Greenwich *v* Chelsea Hospital Pensioners Match' and is dated 1825 (*see page 55*). In the past it has been attributed to Henry Alken Junior (H.G.), but the date – from the years when Alken Senior was producing his best work – and the picture's great quality would suggest that it was by his far more talented father. Much of H.G.'s work is clear imitation of his father's. The picture is in soft pencil and watercolour – Alken's favourite medium – and fortunately most of the original colour is preserved, which gives it additional life. Its quality lies in its fluidity and sense of movement, which is instantly projected.

Alken is best known as a sporting artist, principally for his hunting scenes, but this picture confirms the opinion of many critics that his work is far more closely part of late eighteenth-century caricature than the often amusing but – in comparison – sometimes tame and lifeless sporting art of the nineteenth century. It is revealing to compare this masterly cartoon with a far less accomplished scene of a one-arm and one-leg match, also attributed to H. Alken (*see page 55*). It would seem most likely that this is the work of H. G. Alken, although neither the attribution nor the date is certain.

Caricaturing one-arm and one-leg cricket matches was popular for a limited period of time, but one constant vein of humour has been the amusement caused by the cricketer of

CONFESSIONS OF A DUFFER
'I was ever tempted to whack wildly in its direction.'
Linley Sambourne
1892. *Punch*

This original pen and ink drawing has a vitality which Sambourne's work often lost when engraved onto woodblocks for reproduction in *Punch*.

Left
THE TWELVE LABOURS
OF 'ARRY
Fourth labour – 'Arry plays cricket
and "wishes he 'adn't".
Phil May (1864–1903)
1896. *Punch*

Phil May typified bohemian artistic London of the 1890s. One of the most brilliant artists ever to work for *Punch*, he was reputed to have been the only man to sign his name on the underside of the famous table in the *Punch* dining-room. A Yorkshireman with an ashen white face and bizarre pudding-basin haircut, his compulsive drinking led to his premature death, at the age of thirty-nine, from cirrhosis of the liver.

limited – or sometimes negligible – ability. In 1892 Linley Sambourne produced one of the series which were a popular feature of *Punch*, called 'Confessions of a Duffer', one of which was 'The Duffer at Cricket'. With staring eyes the batsman is braced, legs apart, and unbalanced, with his bat high above his head, about to take a swipe at the ball which will probably be his undoing.

During his long association with the magazine, Sambourne became a figure of great influence at *Punch*. Certainly one of his most talented successors, Phil May, acknowledged his debt to the man when he remarked to Leonard Raven Hill, another *Punch* artist, 'All I know I got from Sambourne.' At first the connection between the thorough, precise Sambourne and the erratic genius May seems surprising, and there is no doubt that May's style of drawing was quite individual.

James Thorpe considered him to have been the greatest

Right
ON THE VILLAGE GREEN
Phil May
c. 1900. *Punch*

Bowler: 'Here, I say! I can't see the wicket. How can I bowl to him?'

Umpire: 'Fire away! If you 'it 'im in front it's leg before! If you 'it 'im be'ind it's a wide!'

English humorous artist since George Cruikshank, while for John Geipel, who wrote *The Cartoon*, he was 'unquestionably one of the most influential draughtsmen in the history of humorous illustration'. The great quality of May's draughtsmanship was his economy of line, in contrast to the dense cross-hatching and thick detail of most of his *Punch* contemporaries. This was not the only thing which set his work apart, for May was no respecter of social niceties and his drawings of coster girls and guttersnipes was, as Thorpe comments, 'a reaction against the English gentlemanly tradition in humorous art which *Punch* had incarnated'.

At one stage in his career May went to Australia, where he worked for the *Sydney Bulletin*. An exchange he had with the editor of the paper shows the importance the artist attached to his style of drawing. 'Of course your work is awfully clever but, I say, you know, we're paying you an enormous salary – and that last drawing of yours – why, there were only seven lines in it.' May's succinct retort was, 'My dear man, don't you realize that if I could have done it with five, I'd have charged you twice as much?'

Some of May's best work was done for different series to appear in the *Punch* Almanacks, which the magazine started up as a polite skit on the more serious, weighty annuals, such as *Whitaker*'s, and which took a light-hearted look at the year to come. The first of May's series appeared in the Almanack for 1896. Called 'The Twelve Labours of 'Arry', it had cartoons for the twelve months of the year, each with the incompetent 'Arry taking part in the sport of the season. Cricket is the fourth labour – April.

One important thing the picture revealed was May's shaky knowledge of some of the finer points of field-placing – which did not escape the eye of W. G. Grace. So concerned was the 'Champion' that he despatched a telegram to the *Punch* office: 'Why, oh why, does square leg wear wicket-keeping gloves?' The message arrived while May was in the middle of a *Punch* dinner, not something that he would allow to be disturbed lightly. He waited until dinner was over before sending his reply, to read which Grace was awakened in the early hours of the morning: 'To keep his hands warm'.

In a second cricket cartoon from a few years later, called 'On the Village Green', May would appear to have brushed up his grasp of the game, for there are no similar errors. The picture is an ideal example of the sort of theme that had

PREHISTORIC PEEPS
'How's that, umpire?'
E. T. Reed
1896. *Punch*

E. T. Reed, an Old Harrovian, was one of the most eccentric *Punch* artists although this was often disguised as most of his work was political or social caricature. His series 'Prehistoric Peeps', a kind of 1890's equivalent of the 'Flintstones', became so popular that it was published as a book in 1896.

become constantly played upon in cartoons of the game: an inordinately fat and obstinate-looking batsman, facing a thin little amateur bowler with specs who attempts to intimidate the umpire (also fat).

One of May's more original contemporary artists was Edward Tennyson Reed, who once commented upon his chosen career: 'I attribute my becoming a caricaturist, in preference to following other walks of life, to the fact that I fell over the banisters at the age of five and landed on my head in a marble hall.'

Starting in 1893, Reed produced an extremely popular series for *Punch* called 'Prehistoric Peeps'. The whole series, many of them illustrating sporting pastimes, fed upon the widespread public speculation and scepticism which had been aroused by Charles Darwin's *On the Origin of Species*. The highly imaginative cricket match, where one of the cavemen playing is clearly recognizable as Grace, shows the diversity of the artist, most of whose work was political but who also

produced witty and elegant parodies of the aesthetes of the period.

Reed's cartoon may contain a hint of fantasy, but the work of Fred Leist, who worked for the *Graphic* between 1901 and 1910 and who produced a series (not for the paper) called 'The Cricketer's Nightmare', takes the discomfort that cricketers all experience at some time to a horrific extreme. The wicket-keeper (*see page 105*) who has just missed the ball, is surrounded by a sea of baying hostility which, one feels, would deter anyone from playing, or at least keeping wicket, ever again.

The work of Frank Reynolds represents a return to normality and to a *Punch* artist who, more than any of the others, was a devoted lover of cricket. In fact, Reynolds worked for *Punch* only after he had been on both the *Illustrated London News* and the *Sketch*, but his double association with the magazine – as artist and then art editor – made him a figure of important influence. One of the most facile and funniest artists to work for the magazine during his art editorship – Fougasse – clearly recognized Reynolds' influence: 'He played, in fact, an important part in the transition from the comparatively tight, naturalistic drawing of the beginning of the century (a legacy from the old wood engraving) to the freer and more fluid and very much less documented styles that followed.'

Much of Reynolds' cricket output was along the fairly well-trodden paths of club or village cricket gaffes with witty captions. At times he produced marvellous caricatures, such as in his series of leading artists of the day in suitable cricketing poses. But it is in comparatively simple pen and ink sketches, such as his two slip-fielders, that his technique is best seen and his humour best displayed. Like most good cartoons it is such a simple idea and a scene which occurs on every cricket field at some time, and the six vignettes of the two absolute 'types' of fielders are more enjoyable than much of Reynolds' more large-scale work.

Reynolds' period as art editor saw the association with *Punch* of H. M. Bateman, an artist who has become probably the best known and most popular in England this century. *Punch* was only one of the periodicals for which he worked during his long career, which began before the First World War and ended after the Second. He died in 1969, aged eighty-three.

TWO MEN IN THE SLIPS
Frank Reynolds (1876–1953)

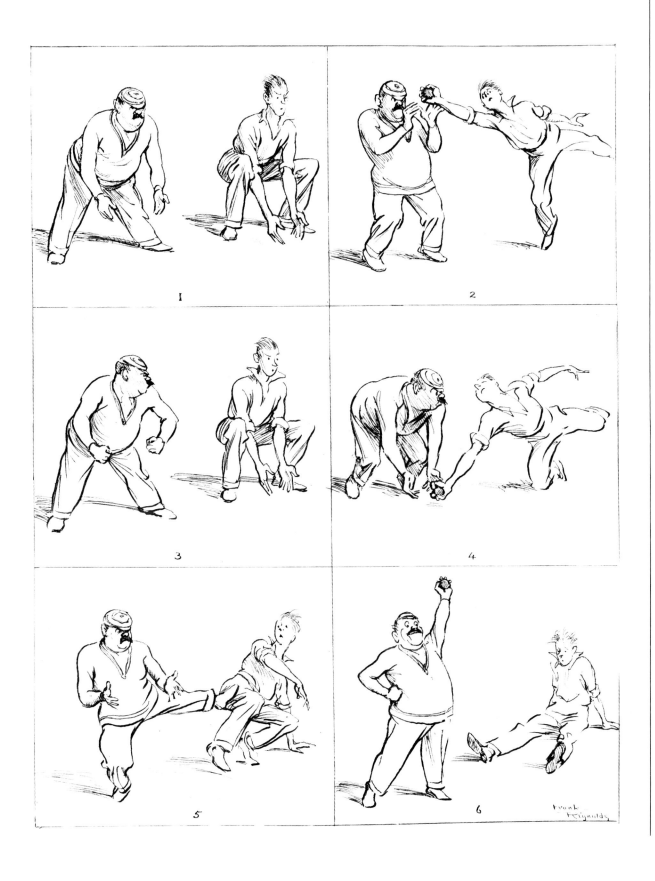

IT'S ALL IN A GAME
H. M. Bateman (1887–1969)
1920. *Punch*

In the *Dictionary of British Book Illustrators and Carica-turists 1800–1914*, Simon Houfe maintains that 'Bateman revolutionized humorous art in Britain making it spontaneous, hilarious and economical.' His critics have argued that he developed a style and theme from which, once established, he rarely diverted, and as a result both his art and humour have a sameness and lack of scope. While this may be true, there is no denying that Bateman struck a vein of humour with enormous appeal. It is essentially English in its pre-occupation with sport, clubs, the army, nannies, and other well-known aspects of the national way of life – as well as specific English social events such as Royal Ascot – and is middle-class in its obsession with doing the right thing, avoiding a *faux pas* which could cause ruin, and laughing at those who do make them.

Bateman may have found a basic theme and stuck to it, but his humour was instantly recognizable and enjoyable. Stylistically his work had the vital ingredient of exaggeration and a series of characteristic touches which became almost Bateman trademarks – teeth being ground in rage, hair standing on end, and the furious frown. One of his best known and most successful styles was the strip without words, which sometimes developed over three or four pages. Most often the theme is of something that starts well, perhaps gets better, but then takes a turn for the worse and finally ends in disaster. His cartoon 'It's All in a Game' is in exactly this style – with the additional theme of how the mighty are fallen, another Bateman favourite.

Contemporary with Bateman was one of England's most inventive humorous artists, William Heath Robinson. If he has become best known for the series of gadgets for which his name has been adopted as a generic label, the scope of Heath Robinson's art was extraordinary. While his fertile imagination produced a never-ending stream of ideas for comedy, his technique was equally diverse and always ensured that his pictures were exquisitely well produced. On some occasions nothing seemed too ridiculous to appeal to Heath Robinson for illustration, and part of his genius was taking the ridiculous to the limits of humour without ever allowing it to become stupid. At other times, however, a cartoon was built around the simplest of ideas.

Both 'Comfortable Cricket' and his cartoon of the crushed worm are ridiculous situations and yet they are wonderfully

COMFORTABLE CRICKET
W. Heath Robinson (1872–1944)

Above
RAGAMUFFINS
G. L. Stampa (1875–1951)
1932

funny. Together they show Heath Robinson's breadth of style, the former with the people and gadgets who appeared regularly in his cartoons, the latter (*see page 106*) quite different and an unusually constructed picture with an over-sized feature at each corner and the main character and focus, the unfortunate baby worm, almost obscured beneath the fallen stump.

'Betcher five pounds I git yer aht this over.'
''Ow much yer got.'
'Three a' pence.'
'Or right I'll betcher.'

Compared with the work of both Bateman and Heath Robinson, that of another inter-war artist, G. L. Stampa, looks decidedly old-fashioned, and indeed Stampa, a bohemian character who modelled himself on an earlier *Punch* artist, Charles Keene, spent much of his time trying to relive the 1890s. In *A History of Punch*, R. G. G. Price described how his determination to live in the past involved 'refusing to have a newspaper or to recognize any change since . . . (the date varied from conversation to conversation)'.

Stampa's cartoon of urchins with tatty boots and cloth caps shows instant evidence of the influence of Phil May, although as an artist he was not in May's class. All the same, his boys,

Right
WILLIE QUAIFE AT THE OVAL
Tom Webster
1925. *Daily Mail*

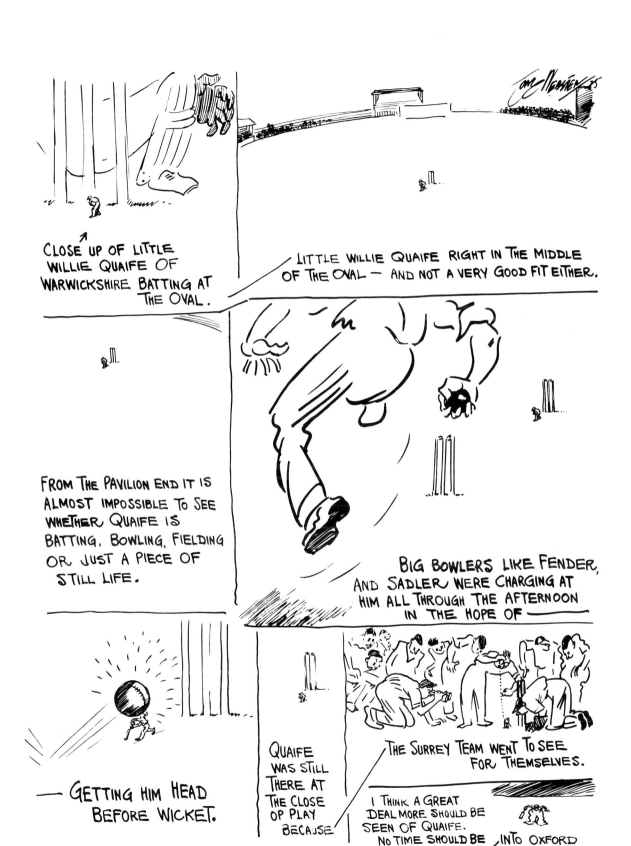

CLOSE UP OF LITTLE WILLIE QUAIFE OF WARWICKSHIRE BATTING AT THE OVAL.

LITTLE WILLIE QUAIFE RIGHT IN THE MIDDLE OF THE OVAL — AND NOT A VERY GOOD FIT EITHER.

FROM THE PAVILION END IT IS ALMOST IMPOSSIBLE TO SEE WHETHER QUAIFE IS BATTING, BOWLING, FIELDING OR JUST A PIECE OF STILL LIFE.

BIG BOWLERS LIKE FENDER, AND SADLER WERE CHARGING AT HIM ALL THROUGH THE AFTERNOON IN THE HOPE OF ——

— GETTING HIM HEAD BEFORE WICKET.

QUAIFE WAS STILL THERE AT THE CLOSE OF PLAY BECAUSE

THE SURREY TEAM WENT TO SEE FOR THEMSELVES.

I THINK A GREAT DEAL MORE SHOULD BE SEEN OF QUAIFE. NO TIME SHOULD BE LOST IN PUTTING HIM — INTO OXFORD TROUSERS.

THE FAST BOWLER
James Thorpe

An interesting cartoon for James Thorpe who rarely used exaggeration, preferring to convey his humour by a combination of the antics of the people in his cartoons and a witty caption.

their makeshift games of cricket and their rivalry could be found anywhere, both during Stampa's life and before or afterwards.

The cricketers and cricket scenes depicted by various *Punch* artists were generally 'types' – albeit modelled on real people – for they were commenting upon English life in general rather than the events of the day. For a newspaper cartoonist such as Tom Webster the daily sporting events were his bread and butter, and his supreme quality was evidenced by the limitless ways he had of presenting a day's cricket. In 1925 he produced a cartoon after a day's play at The Oval which, as well as giving an accurate outline of what happened, also presents the situation of an oppressed batsman quite brilliantly.

The images of Warwickshire's tiny hero Quaife (who played over 600 matches for the county and did not retire until he was fifty-six), towered over by the stumps and wicket-keeper, marooned in the centre of the enormous field and threatened by the vast figure of the approaching bowler, show Webster at his comic best, describing actual events at the same time as making a wider comment on the game.

The fearsome fast bowler is one of the best-known humorous characters on the cricket field and he appears at every level of the game, from the village green (the blacksmith in A. G. Macdonell's *England Their England*) to Test cricket. James Thorpe's cartoon shows him as he appears to many batsmen, especially the less competent ones – outsize and devilish, about to hand out their unhappy fate.

The second cartoon is in all ways more characteristic of Thorpe and shows the bowler in a rather different light. Gently amusing and nothing more or less than a humorous observation, the cartoon appears rather bland today but would no doubt have appealed to club cricketers all over the country who had experienced a similar situation.

One of the most popular aspects of cartoons in daily newspapers has been the characters they have created and their regular appearance in an ever-changing role. Reg Wootton's Sporting Sam, who appeared for many years in the *Sunday Express*, has been one of the most lovable of the post-war period. Always keen, optimistic and over-helpful, Sam's prowess at the various sports never quite came up to scratch. But whether he is playing or just being his obliging self – as here – the essence of the cartoon is one simple joke.

'A cricketer can do this all day.

THE CRICKET BAG
James Thorpe
1921. *Punch*

But five minutes of this reduces him
to a state of pulp.'

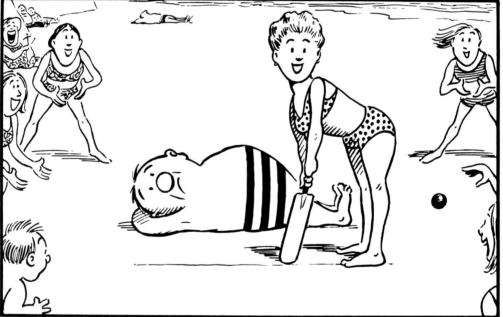

SPORTING SAM
Reg Wootton

CHAPTER FIVE

The Umpires

In cricket's very earliest days there were no umpires at all. Disputes on the field were resolved by a senior player or spectator – probably the aristocrat who had organized the game or who, by the seniority of his social position, commanded an authority which nobody dared to question. By the time of the MCC's foundation, however, umpires had become a compulsory and accepted part of cricket, and if their job has adapted over the years to the changing face of the game, the basic priorities of their position, as well as the problems inherent in it, have hardly altered.

Despite the weight given to their position on paper, few people would deny that the umpires' job can be relentlessly exacting. Authority and impartiality may be the two keystones of umpiring, but in a game of such complexity as cricket success at the job also calls for intuitive judgement and deep knowledge of the game. In the old days umpires were armed with a stick, not primarily as a weapon but because the batsmen had to touch the stick to complete a run. But in a tight spot when a knife-edge decision had to be made it was reassuring support, and no doubt some of the more volatile umpires had no qualms about using it.

Today the umpire has no such means of self-protection or of establishing his authority, and there is little doubt that the task has become more difficult and demanding. This is particularly true at the highest level as a result of the assessing powers of television and radio which can undermine the authority of an umpire by questioning his decision. And such questioning on the field, as well as deliberate intimidation, has certainly become more widespread – although not even the most ardent supporter of the 'good old days' would deny that it happened in the past: the great W.G. himself was at times a shameless bully of umpires. More basic is the problem found at all levels of cricket of players being unwilling to accept the authority of an umpire and therefore to accept a decision with which they disagree.

All the same, an umpire's job is not unmitigated woe. The best umpires have invariably been those who, as well as their other qualities, have kept one step ahead of the players and as a result have been able to see the funny side of their job. Taken at a lighter level than those decisions upon which the whole prestige of nation, village or club may hang, it is a position on the field with as much humorous potential as any other. It is also because the umpires are quite different from the playing protagonists in a game of cricket, and yet play a decisive role, that they have been afforded a chapter of their own.

In club and village cricket, where one umpire is often a club's ageing secretary or president whose playing days are over, or a loyal and respected member of the home team's community, impartiality often takes second place and a host

TWO UMPIRES
Tom Webster
1924. *Weekly Dispatch*

'These gentlemen went out into the field yesterday for four months complete rest. They will not be woken up until the end of August and only the tea intervals will disturb them.'

of tricks – deafness, temporary unsighting, etc. – come into play. When his partner is a member of the batting side – and often a junior one at that – the need for this unfortunate to avoid giving out one of his own side can produce hilarious results. Together the two officials can cause uproar.

A leading sports cartoonist such as Tom Webster, whose job was to provide his journal with continuous daily comment on the sporting calendar, would always be looking for subjects for cartoon. Also, he was in a position to exploit any opportunity of making fun of umpires in the same way as he lampooned the players. Sometimes the opportunities presented themselves in actual matches, and an umpiring decision or incident which provided a highlight in a day's Test cricket would not have escaped his notice.

In 1924 Webster used the occasion of the opening of the season to produce a delightful caricature of umpires and of their job. It was drawn for the *Weekly Despatch* (part of the same group as the *Daily Mail* and renamed the *Sunday Despatch* in 1928). The two contrasting figures capture brilliantly the popular idea of umpires as universally elderly and sleepy.

Two years before Webster drew his cartoon a young man (aged twenty-six) called Frank Chester, who had played for Worcestershire before the First World War, began his career as a first-class umpire. Chester turned to umpiring as a result of the loss of his right arm during the war. During the next thirty years he transformed the position, not only by the standards he set but also because he was the first person to rise above the umpire's usual anonymity and become a cricketing personality. Umpiring became his career, and the novelty of his appearance was evident in the fact that most of his fellow umpires were usually twice his age.

If Chester was the first umpire to become a well-known personality in the cricketing world, the best known of his successors have been Sid Buller, who just overlapped with Chester for a few years, and more recently, Dickie Bird. Bird in particular has managed to combine complete authority and fine judgement with a lively, individual sense of humour which has particularly endeared him to players and crowds alike.

None of these three would have allowed himself to get into such a dreadful, compromising situation as the one which is the subject of one of H. M. Bateman's best cricketing car-

NOT OUT?
Umpire: 'Not out wasn't yer? Well you wait till you see the evening paper!'
James Thorpe
c. 1920. *Punch*

toons, 'The Umpire Who Confessed He Wasn't Looking' (*see page 107*). The cartoon pinpoints and exploits the momentary lapse, in the best Bateman tradition which also inspired his 'The Man Who . . .' series as well as hosts of other cartoons with the same theme. The poor umpire has neither friend nor supporter in sight – the only possible ally, his partner at square leg, is not in view, although it is likely that even he may have had scant sympathy. The fielders and spectators are in uproar and even the non-striking batsman, whose team might benefit from the mistake, cannot conceal his incredulous enjoyment of such an unforgivable error.

Unlike most of the other cartoons by Bateman on this theme, where onlookers crowd in on the wretched creature who has perpetrated the crime, here the sense of open space cleverly heightens the umpire's pathetic isolation. It is the greatly exaggerated features of the one fielder in the foreground that ensure that the cartoon's message is conveyed instantaneously.

Bateman's cartoon makes great mockery of an umpiring mistake, but an earlier cartoon by Fred Leist transports the mockery into the realm of nightmare. It is one of his series called 'The Cricketer's Nightmare' and, like all the others, is funny in a rather chilling way. The cartoon focuses on the awful dilemma upon whose horns umpires are often impaled, especially those lacking in either confidence or expertise, where he knows that whatever decision he makes – and he is not even certain which is the right one – it is going to antagonize one party or the other (*see page 107*).

One of the best-known comic situations involving umpires was illustrated in a cartoon by James Thorpe. As the obviously disgruntled batsman passes the umpire on his way back to the pavilion he makes it clear that he feels hard done by in the decision that ended his innings. Unmoved, and secure in the knowledge of his authority, the umpire replies with finality, 'Oh not out wasn't yer? Well wait till you see the evening paper.' How often umpires at all levels of cricket must feel like saying that to an outgoing batsman who, even if he says nothing, has made it clear by his antics or expression that he disagrees with a decision.

In another cartoon Thorpe depicts a situation whose humour is reminiscent of P. G. Wodehouse, and one can almost hear the immortal Jeeves uttering just such a line as that of the impassive chauffeur. As a cartoon it is a delightful

period piece – the squire unashamedly coercing his employee and stressing the social superiority which he takes for granted by adding the latter's surname to his appeal.

Disagreements between players and umpires at the level of club and village cricket may arouse strong feelings in the short term, but they are usually kept well in check and washed away with a drink in the pub afterwards, the opposing parties finishing the day on cordial terms. At the level of Test cricket, however, especially in recent years, real acrimony has at times boiled to the surface and players have shown an unedifying lack of both self-control and respect for the umpire's authority. Stumps have been kicked over by enraged bowlers or knocked over by batsmen unable to accept an umpire's verdict, and verbal abuse of umpires has come from batsmen, bowlers and fielders alike.

As far as English cricketers are concerned, things had never

HOW'S THAT?
Square leg: 'How's that Collins?'
His Chauffeur: 'Practically
simultaneous, Sir.'
James Thorpe
1921. *Punch*

approached the nadir they reached in Pakistan in 1987, in an incident which provided John Jensen with the material for a graphic cartoon for *Punch* – as it did cartoonists for virtually every newspaper and magazine. England's captain, Mike Gatting, indulged in an ugly verbal and physical confrontation on the field with a Pakistani umpire, Shakoor Rana, which almost caused a diplomatic incident and did grievous harm to the reputations of the game in general and modern players in particular.

After their return home, the England players had a short break before setting off for a tour of New Zealand, from which they made a short trip to Melbourne for a Test celebrating Australia's bicentenary. Without apportioning blame for the incident in Pakistan, Jensen uses the forthcoming trip to Australia to illustrate the depths to which things had sunk and how they would further deteriorate if such confrontations were to continue (*see page 108*). The humour of the cartoon and the ridiculous, exaggerated expressions of both player and umpire put out a depressing message and offer a serious and timely warning.

Incidents such as this have been mercifully rare, but they illustrate to what extent, in the commercial and competitive climate of the modern game, umpires have become vulnerable: a flash-point which in the past might have brought a caustic jibe or humorous aside now results in outright aggression. Happily, humorous recollections or illustrations of the umpire's task greatly outnumber the unfortunate ones for the vast majority of cricket enthusiasts. As we have seen, the potential for personal idiosyncracy in umpires and the comic side of many of the positions in which they find themselves normally lie only just below the surface of the game, and it would be a tragedy if the amusing aspect of umpiring were to be squeezed out.

CHAPTER SIX

Spectators

No game of cricket is complete without spectators who, coming in all shapes and sizes, are often more revealing about the character of a match than the actual players. From the usually exclusively male, stovepipe-hatted groups of the early nineteenth century, many of whom would have laid a wager on the game's outcome, to the voluble, bare-torsoed occupants of Sydney's Hill, the appearance and behaviour of spectators have reflected the societies of different periods.

It was primarily the matches at Lord's, organized or played by the MCC, which were responsible for giving cricket a social importance which grew steadily through the nineteenth century. Ground and club are the subject of a later chapter, so suffice it to say here that crowds at Lord's have usually been – at least until recent years – the most decorative, society-orientated and, many people would argue, socially self-conscious to be found anywhere.

If no ground can match the social importance of Lord's, one county ground whose midsummer week of county cricket has always been a social occasion is Canterbury. Cricket has a longer history in Kent than anywhere else, going back to the early eighteenth century, so by the beginning of the nineteenth century it was well established on grounds around the county, many of which were at the seats of leading families. Thereafter the establishment of two clubs, the Band of Brothers and I Zingari (although not a Kent club it has always had strong affiliations with the county), cemented the links between cricket and society. The Canterbury Week began in 1842 and was an occasion for cricket during the day and theatricals during the evening, performed by the Old Stagers many of whom became original members of I Zingari on its foundation in 1845.

The theatricals and social importance have remained, but it was during the 1890s, when the county's first-class cricket

THE WICKET-KEEPER
Fred Leist (career 1901–10)
c. 1905

Little is known about the artist Fred Leist, which only adds to the effect of his weird series 'The Cricketer's Nightmare'.

THE UMPIRE WHO CONFESSED
HE WASN'T LOOKING
H. M. Bateman

Opposite

THE CRICKET MATCH
'The mother earth worm to its
wormlet – now then Florizel, that just
serves you right, – how often have I
told you to keep away from the wicket
during these Test Matches.'
W. Heath Robinson
1926. *The Bystander*

Heath Robinson was not only humorous but a highly skilled and original
artist, as shown in the construction of
this picture. The heavy detail in the four
corners and the dark shadows greatly
increase the impact of the fate of the
crushed wormlet.

Right
THE UMPIRE
Fred Leist
c. 1905

Above
GATTING AND AN AUSTRALIAN
UMPIRE
John Jensen
1987. *Punch*

One of the most notorious incidents of
modern Test cricket, the row between
England's captain Gatting and the
Pakistani umpire, Shakoor Rana,
prompted this cartoon by Jensen, an-
ticipating England's progress from
Pakistan to Australia.

Right
ENGLAND v AUSTRALIA, LORD'S
1972
Roy Ullyett
1972

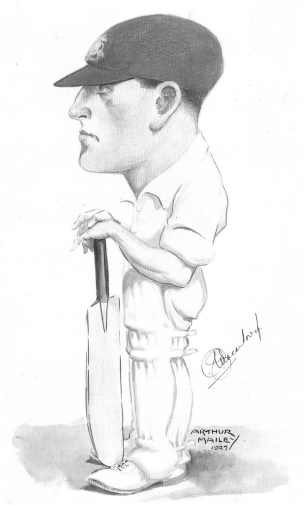

Right
C. G. MACARTNEY (1886–1958)
A. A. Mailey
1926

Above left
LILLEE'S APPROACH
Ralph Steadman
1977. *The Listener*

Below left
HOWZAT!
Ralph Steadman
1977. *The Listener*

Above
MEDIA INTEREST 1986
John Jensen
1986. *Punch*

R. A. FITZGERALD
Alfred Bryan
1874

Above
CANTERBURY WEEK
Sydney Higham (career 1890–1905)
c. 1890. *The Graphic*

Sydney Higham's delightful series of pen and ink sketches is a good example of the pre-eminence that black and white artists of his calibre still enjoyed in all departments of the newspaper world at the end of the 19th century, as yet unthreatened by the challenge of photography.

was embarking upon its most successful period, that, under the controlling eye of Lord Harris, Canterbury Week approached its zenith. The scene was portrayed by Sydney Higham in the *Graphic* with a series of pen and ink sketches. The elegant artistry of the vignettes is complemented by the gentle humour of the captions such as 'Thorough Sportsmen' and 'Another Boundary – Two Versions', and the picture is a delightful evocation of the period, wittily highlighting the stalwarts ignoring the rain, the top-hatted gentlemen and the more flamboyantly dressed ladies.

Certainly during the nineteenth century it was cricket as a social occasion which was its primary attraction for ladies and this is illustrated in a cartoon by George du Maurier, *Punch*'s foremost cartoonist of Victorian high society. Du Maurier was born in Paris where he studied to become an artist, but the

loss of one eye ended his ambitions to paint. Turning exclusively to black and white work, he came to London in 1860
and produced occasional drawings for *Punch* until 1864 when
he succeeded John Leech as the main commentator upon
fashion and society.

Although du Maurier never became the magazine's first
artist, his importance was enormous and for many years the
popularity of his work was vital to the circulation. One
contribution to the fashion world with which du Maurier was
credited was the creation of the tall woman, in full-length
dresses, with a swan-like neck and swept-up hair, who came
to epitomize the elegance of late Victorian and Edwardian
society.

In du Maurier's cartoon Lady Mildmay and her companion
are sitting, but her elegance is obvious even from behind. In
addition to being an illustration of fashion, the picture's
caption makes fun of feminine ignorance of the niceties of
cricket in a manner that was repeated half a century later by
James Thorpe. It is interesting that Thorpe adopts the same
technique as du Maurier, of presenting the back views of the
two characters in his cartoon. He also makes sure that his

Right
A LITTLE LEARNING
James Thorpe
1928. *Punch*

The Man: 'That fellow's getting all his
runs on the off side.'
The Woman: 'Yes dear, I can't think
why the umpire doesn't blow his
whistle.'

Below
LADY MILDMAY
'By the way – a – are they playing
"Rugby" or "Association"!'
George du Maurier (1834–96)
c. 1875

George du Maurier was first and foremost an observer of fashionable society
and one of the best who ever worked
for *Punch*. His admiration of Linley
Sambourne – he considered Sambourne
the only man he knew capable of drawing a top hat properly – reflects his
priorities as an artist.

Left
THE COLLECTOR
James Thorpe
1929. *Passing Show*

Fairly Distinguished Cricketer: 'But I've signed your book before.'

The Collector: 'Yes sir, when I get eight of yours I can swap 'em for one of Hobbs.'

Below
SUPERIORITY
The boy that threw up from the boundary the ball that Hobbs hit.
G. L. Stampa
1927

illustration is sufficiently flattering for the lady's comment to come over as charming innocence rather than unacceptable ignorance – which such a remark would undoubtedly have reflected coming from a man.

The society lady has been one 'type' of cricket spectator to have provided rich material for the pens of cricket caricaturists. Another has been the small boy whose life is filled with cricketing heroes and dreams of playing for his village, county or even country. From cricket's earliest days they have been found at all types of matches, occasionally as players bamboozling their elders, but more often practising on the boundary, filling in scorebooks or pursuing the age-old pastime of collecting autographs.

The serious business of autograph-hunting which, for the dedicated expert, gives players different values to be bought and sold like any other commodity, is captured perfectly by Thorpe in another cartoon. Here is the ultimate put-down for the club cricketer, who in the picture is looking condescendingly at the schoolboy brandishing his book and pen, both in his being described by Thorpe as a '*fairly* distinguished cricketer', and in the collector's reply to the complaint that he

NOBBY
'Never misses a match, Nobby don't
– loves it 'e does. I'll bet 'e's dreamin'
about cricket now.'
G. L. Stampa
1936

had already signed his name: 'Yes sir, when I get eight of yours I can swap 'em for one of Hobbs.'

For most small boys between the wars Jack Hobbs was a god-like figure, leagues ahead of virtually all other players in prowess, popularity and reputation. Reading H. S. Altham's description in *Barclays World of Cricket*, this was hardly surprising:

But it is not only for his prowess on the field that he will be remembered with such admiration and affection by all who knew him. A man of natural dignity, with at the same time an engaging twinkle that revealed a charming and constant sense of humour, [he was] utterly unspoilt by success and always prepared to help others, especially the young . . .

Thorpe's cartoon points to Hobbs' great reputation among small boys, as does another produced at about the same time by George Stampa, although in a different manner. The stylistic contrast between the two cartoons shows immediately the differences between Thorpe, whose characters usually came from polite society, and Stampa, whose urchins were figures from the street scenes of his mentor, Phil May. In Stampa's picture it is the crushing superiority of the boy who has actually touched a ball hit by Hobbs, to the envious astonishment of his fellows, which makes the cartoon.

Stampa's style was well suited to the scene of village cricket where the dozing figure of a local habitué has always been a well-known sight. Since cricket was first played, on hard benches under trees old-timers who have often never wielded a cricket bat in their lives have slept off the after-effects of a few lunch-time pints of beer, and there is hardly a village ground that does not have one. If the humour is somewhat predictable, this is the atmosphere which Stampa captures with his cartoon and accompanying caption.

The *habitué* of the village green might often be a primarily sleepy onlooker, but the dedicated cricket spectator is very different. Wherever he is to be found he displays instantly recognizable characteristics: quiet resignation and patience, thorough preparation shown by the assembled mackintosh, newspaper, packed lunch, thermos flask, sun-hat, pen and book, and a devotion to the slow-moving ebb and flow of a game of cricket which enables him to sit happily enjoying and analysing through hours or even days of play. In addition he is tenacious, quite prepared to put up with a certain degree of discomfort, and there is little that will put him off attending. This grim stoicism is captured in Tom Webster's cartoon 'The Man Who is Really Entitled to the Ashes'.

Weather, particularly rainy weather, which plays such havoc with cricket fixtures, was one of Webster's favourite subjects and something he used with regular hilarity. This cartoon appeared in the *Daily Mail* in August 1926, at the end of a Test series which had been plagued by rain, not least the final match at The Oval, which produced the only result – an England victory, bringing back the Ashes for the first time since the First World War. But like all of Webster's cartoons which do not comment upon a specific situation or player, the humour is timeless, as relevant today as it was sixty years ago.

Webster's cartoon shows one kind of cricket stalwart. Another – or rather a pair of others – appears in a cartoon by Fougasse who was an almost exact contemporary of Webster's and, in his quite different way, equally brilliant. Fougasse's real name was Cyril Kenneth Bird, but when he embarked upon his career as a cartoonist there was already an artist working for *Punch* who used the *nom de plume* W. Bird.

THE
MAN
WHO
IS
REALLY
ENTITLED
"TO
THE ASHES"

IN
SITTING
THROUGH
ALL FIVE
TEST MATCHES
HE HAS GONE
THROUGH
HAIL, RAIN,
FOG. SNOW,
VERY LITTLE SUN
AND LOTS OF
LIGHTNING.

ALTOGETHER, HE HAS
GIVEN A MARVELLOUS
EXHIBITION OF
PERFECT SPECTATORSHIP.

THE MAN WHO IS REALLY
ENTITLED TO THE ASHES
Tom Webster
1926. *Daily Mail*

The 'fougasse' from which Bird took his name was a kind of French mine used in the First World War, but it is uncertain whether he chose the name because he had been blown up at Gallipoli in 1915 or because, as Bevis Hillier maintains in his book on the artist, 'a "fougasse" was a French mine, a rough and ready affair which might or might not go off: Kenneth Bird modestly thought the same was true of his cartoons.' Prevented by his injuries from taking up his chosen career as an engineer, Fougasse turned to drawing, for which he had already shown a talent. In 1916 he took a correspondence course in illustration and in the same year his first cartoon appeared in *Punch*.

Fougasse argued that a good cartoonist had to have a sense of humour first and draughtsmanship second, and this was true in his own case. The originality of his work lay in its spareness: the minimum of lines necessary to give the desired effect. Such was the humour of his ideas before they were put on to paper that he was able to project them in a very simplistic manner. Exaggeration beyond an outsize grin or hair standing on end was rarely used.

It is interesting to compare Fougasse with Bateman, both drawing for *Punch* at the same time. There are similarities in much of the situation comedy they illustrate, in particular the social embarrassment which their audiences found so unfailingly funny. In fact, people have argued that it was Fougasse who first produced 'The Man Who . . .' and that Bateman took it up subsequently. But the differences easily outweigh the similarities. Compared with Bateman's instant hilarity, Fougasse's wit is as restrained as his drawing technique, at times whimsical, at others quietly making fun of the cautious lives most people live.

One young artist whom Fougasse greatly admired and who was retained by *Punch* for a few years before the Second World War was Graham Laidler, or 'Pont'. Pont's life ended in his tragically premature death at the age of thirty-two in 1940, but in his short career he enjoyed huge popularity, principally for his series produced during the 1930s called 'The British Character', which caricatured those peculiarly British loves, hatreds, phobias, talents to be admired and situations to be avoided.

One of the series was called 'Fondness for Cricket', which appeared in *Punch* in 1937. Showing as it does passengers leaning out of the windows of a train to catch even the smallest

Left
TWO SPECTATORS
'Of course there's one thing no
foreigner will ever understand, and
that's our enthusiasm for cricket.'
Fougasse
1922. *Punch*

The cartoon of two spectators in a huge
empty stand is a perfect example of
Fougasse at his most understated.
Theirs is the mildly prejudiced self-
confidence which typified the English
middle classes between the wars and
which at times was easy to make look
ridiculous.

Right
FONDNESS OF CRICKET
Graham Laidler. 'Pont'. (1908–40)
1937. *Punch*

In his introduction to a book of Pont's
work published in 1942 after his death,
Fougasse points to the skill required to
achieve the desired effect of the cartoon. 'A drawing of a railway train, for
instance, travelling along an embank-
ment as it passes a cricket ground with
a match in progress, would present
almost insuperable difficulties to the
average humorous artist and especially
to the tolerably good one – not so Pont,
whose drawing of the scene gives the
illusion (for illusion it must be) that
he has started straight off with a pen
without any preliminary pencil and
rubber, and has filled the whole thing
without a pause or hesitation.'

For an artist like Fougasse, who once
remarked that he used the rubber more
than the pencil, the sense of spontaneity
and immediacy about Pont's cartoon
must have been all the more impressive.

glimpse of a game of cricket as they rush past, one feels that it
must have been inspired by a passage in Neville Cardus's
Cricket, published in 1930:

Has any true Englishman ever resisted the temptation, while
travelling on the railway, to look through the carriage window
whenever the train has been passing a cricket field? The train rushes
round a curve just as the bowler is about to bowl; in a flash we are
swept out of sight of the game, and never know what happened to
that ball!

The sort of devotees illustrated by Webster, Fougasse, Pont
and many other English cartoonists have been a constant

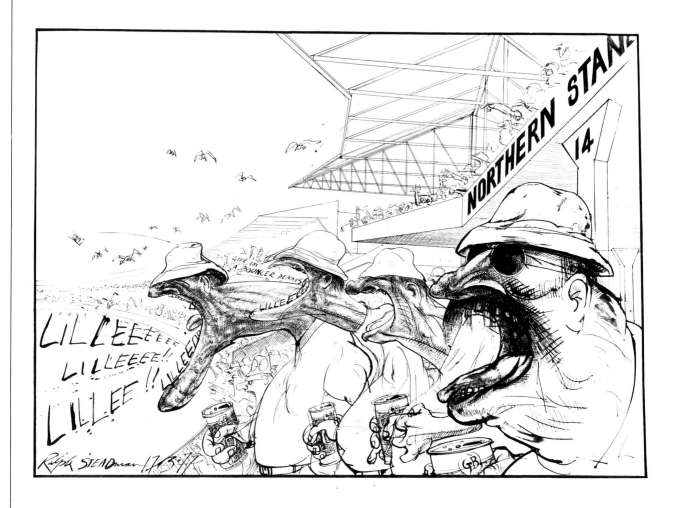

feature of cricket in this country since its inception. They are
the living evidence of the nation's fascination with the game –
the people for whom cricket (to use a well-worn cliché) is not
just a game but a way of life.

Also devoted, or rather, fanatical in a manner which traditional supporters find alarming, is the modern Australian
spectator illustrated by Ralph Steadman in a cartoon of the
Centenary Test between Australia and England at Melbourne
in 1977. The devotion of these spectators is not to the game in
general and the pastime of cricket-watching, but to their hero,
the Australian fast bowler Dennis Lillee.

The combination of Lillee's devastating bowling and his
aggressive manner had enormous appeal for certain Australian spectators. He was able to fulfil their desire to see batsmen
– especially Englishmen – subjected to fierce assault and
humiliation. It was this aggression by which Steadman – a

AUSTRALIAN SPECTATORS
Ralph Steadman
1977. *The Listener*

relative stranger to cricket – was most struck during his visit to the Centenary Test.

I should say immediately that the modern cricket spectator who is primarily interested in excitement and fast-moving action is by no means an exclusively Australian phenomenon. Today he is to be found at cricket grounds all over the world and it is the enjoyment of these aspects of cricket which accounts for the popularity of the one-day game, whose advent has attracted a quite different type of spectator to the man whose diet was exclusively three-day county games or five-day Tests. As the nature of the game, its surroundings, those who play it and the way it is played alter, so, inevitably, the people who turn up to watch change accordingly.

CHAPTER SEVEN

England v Australia

England *v* Australia is the competition which reigns supreme over cricket, replacing the now defunct Gentlemen *v* Players – it was the initiator of Test cricket, and is now the most senior in both age and importance of international series. Test cricket was played against South Africa shortly after the England *v* Australia matches began, but thereafter no further Test-playing country emerged for forty years. The most significant difference between England *v* Australia and all other Test series, at least during the earlier series, is that whereas with all their other opponents England – if at their full strength – were always the superior side, against Australia they had met their match straight away. With only a few exceptions this situation continued until after the Second World War. For over a hundred years and 250 Test matches the two countries have competed against each other with a determination often charged with intense national pride. As well as producing a greater number of superlative matches than any other Test competition, what has given England *v* Australia Test cricket the edge has been the importance of winning a complete Test series, embodied in the prestige of the Ashes.

The initiation of cricket against Australia, which began with the visit of an English team in 1861, was to have a profound impact upon the game. It had reached a stage of sufficient maturity and confidence in England to feel capable of spreading its wings into an international sphere in such a manner that, in less than twenty years which saw a number of pioneer tours to Australia, the games had become formalized into Test matches. The first three Tests were all played in Australia, two by James Lillywhite's side in 1876–7 and one by Lord Harris's side in 1878–9. During this last match the Australians showed the refreshingly scant respect for their English opponents which has always been part of their attitude to the competitions, by assaulting his lordship during a crowd invasion and subsequent brawl.

More significant than these matches were the first two Australian visits to England, in 1878 and 1880. In 1878 no Test match was played but the Australians caused a sensation by beating the mighty MCC at Lord's. The writing was on the wall, not only after this match but at the end of the tour by which time Australia had lost only four out of twenty eleven-a-side matches played. H. S. Altham commented in *A History of Cricket*: 'The main interest in this first Australian visit lies not so much in the actual record of results, nor even in the shock administered to our insular satisfaction, but in its effect upon the evolution of the game.'

Two years later, at the end of a highly disorganized tour during which the Australians had at times been reduced to advertising for opponents, the first Test match in England was played at The Oval. W. G. Grace – who played with two of his brothers – scored 152, the first Test hundred, and England won by five wickets, although it must be said that Australia were hugely disadvantaged by the absence of the injured Spofforth.

Once begun, England *v* Australia Test cricket leapt forward into a decade of frantic energy. By the end of the 1890 series in England the ten years since the 1880 game had seen as many series; there have never been as many in one decade since. Admittedly many of the programmes involved only one Test match but, considering the travelling involved, it was an extraordinary flowering.

As well as the quantity of cricket, the heights to which it was to rise soon became evident, during the single Test match of 1882. England, with a side of immensely impressive batting ability, were ranged against the Australians dominated by their fast bowling, led by Spofforth. In the event the rain had a decisive influence, and after a final stage of such tension that one spectator was reported to have gnawed lumps out of his umbrella handle, Australia won by 7 runs – Spofforth the hero adding 7 for 44 in the second innings to his 7 for 46 in the first.

This was the Test which gave birth to the Ashes, the *Sporting Life* carrying a notice of the death of English cricket whose 'body will be cremated and the Ashes taken to

Australia'. In the event they stayed there only a few months and were won back by the Hon. Ivo Bligh's side in 1882–3. It was Bligh who was presented with the actual ashes of a bail which have been fought over ever since.

The Australian visit to England of 1884 was of particular significance, both because it was the first time that more than one Test was played in this country, and because it saw the first Test at Lord's. The rubber was won by England, their victory at Lord's being the only result, but Australia ran them extremely close and were definitely on top in the two draws at Old Trafford and The Oval. In the latter match, in an Australian total of 551 their captain Gregory scored the first Test double-century of 211.

A few weeks later, as the Australians were about to leave, their departure was marked in *Ally Sloper's Half Holiday* with Ally Sloper himself saying farewell. Ally's side, Sloper CC, appeared regularly in the pages of the halfpenny weekly, usually with the captain and the motley collection who made up his team performing with hilarious incompetence.

After the furious activity of the 1880s the regularity of England *v* Australia series declined. The standard of play certainly did not, however, and during the 1890s further foundations were laid with the beginning of regular five-match series, the appearance of selection committees for the sides and the establishment of a Board of Control for Test cricket. The first home series of the new century, in 1902, was perhaps the greatest of all time; the Australian team, containing their second generation of outstanding players, such as Trumper, Hill, Noble, Armstrong and Trumble, won 2–1 against England's cream of the Golden Age – including MacLaren, Ranji, Fry, Jackson, Jessop, Hirst and Rhodes.

Thereafter England visited Australia in 1903–4 determined to win back the Ashes, the side captained by P. F. Warner and the tour the first to be undertaken under the official auspices of the MCC. Australia had won the last four series and English prestige was seriously threatened – a strong reason for MCC's involvement. In the event the tour was a triumph, and after winning 3–2 Warner's team returned home with the Ashes after many notable performances, not least Warner's captaincy and R. E. Foster's 287 at Sydney which remained the highest Test score for twenty-five years.

The success was celebrated in a cartoon which is one of the most unusual in the MCC's collection – not on account of its

ALLY SLOPER AND MURDOCH
W. G. Baxter (1856–88)
1884. *Ally Sloper's Half Holiday*

Ally Sloper was the prototype of the heroes of comic strips which were beginning to appear in great numbers at the time. In his capacity as the representative Englishman, Ally Sloper is here bidding farewell to Murdoch and his Australian side.

W. G. Baxter was born in Ireland and later lived in Manchester where he established his own satirical weekly. Moving to London he met Charles Ross, who had recently created Ally Sloper. Taking over the cartoons, Baxter made Ally Sloper into a Victorian legend. He died of consumption in 1888 aged thirty-two.

style but because of its artist, William Slatter. Slatter was one of a family who gave extraordinary service to the MCC at Lord's which he himself estimated to total over two hundred years. His own contribution was fifty-one years, during which time he rose from being a pavilion attendant to Clerk of the Works.

Possibly the most conclusive series victory by Australia against England came with their first visit after the First World War, when they won the first three Tests with embarrassing ease and drew the remaining two. There is no question that their side, captained by Warwick Armstrong and containing batsmen of the calibre of Bardsley and Macartney and the bowling partnership of Gregory and McDonald, was one of formidable strength, and throughout the combative Armstrong gave little quarter.

At the end of the series in August Frank Reynolds, by this time the art editor of *Punch*, produced a cartoon whose style harked back to the days of the magazine's Victorian

Right
THE LION TAMER
'I know a good man when I see one.
Sign, please.'
Frank Reynolds
1921. *Punch*

It is interesting to compare this cartoon by Reynolds, about which everything is in the archetypal, but by this time rather out-dated, style of *Punch*'s full-page cartoons with his far more deft sketches of two slip-fielders on page 85.

Left
HOW ABOUT THOSE ASHES?
'Little Australia/Fearless of failure/
Eating his Test Match tart/He put in his thumb/When out popped a 'Plum'/
And gave him a terrible start.'
William Slatter
1904. *Bystander*

As a devoted supporter of Lord's where Warner played for Middlesex and was a leading MCC figure, Slatter's admiration for 'Plum' is not surprising and the success of Warner's tour to Australia gave him the ideal opportunity to express it.

WELL PLAYED, SIR!
Sidney Strube (1891–1956)
1926. *Daily Express*

stateliness, gravity and ponderous humour. 'The Lion Tamer'
shows the Australian captain about to depart, with the Ashes
safely tucked into his bag, and the humbled English lion
offering up an autograph book with the servile remark, 'I
know a good man when I see one. Sign, please.'

On that 1921 tour one of the great features of the Australian side was the batting of C. G. Macartney – most exhilarating
against Nottinghamshire when he scored 345 runs in a day,
a record that still stands. Macartney often attacked bowlers
mercilessly, making them appear quite ineffective, and something of his pugnacity is discernible in the caricature by his

team-mate, Arthur Mailey, with the emphasis on the jutting chin and cap pulled down hard over the eyes (*see page 108*).

After the success of 1921 Australia defended the Ashes in 1924–5 with an equally resounding series victory of 4–1. When they returned to England in 1926, however, the tables were turned and, after four successive draws, England won convincingly at The Oval and at last regained the Ashes under a newly appointed captain, Percy Chapman, with Wilfred Rhodes recalled aged forty-eight.

The victory was the cause of national celebration of which there was no clearer indication than the cartoon which appeared in the *Daily Express* by 'Strube'. During his thirty-six years with the *Express*, Strube was almost exclusively a political cartoonist for whom sporting events were of little interest. Here, however, is an event of sufficient national importance for his pen, and he illustrates it with his 'little man' cheering the English lion with a smiling Oval gasometer in the background. In the lion's mane are the names of Hobbs and

THE NEXT TEST – AMAZING
SCOOP!
David Low
1933. *Evening Standard*

THE NEXT TEST.– AMAZING SCOOP !

WITH CHARACTERISTIC ENTERPRISE THIS NEWSPAPER HAS ARRANGED WITH THE SUPERNATURAL AUTHORITIES (OLD LOW, LOCAL AGENT) TO PRESENT THESE SNAPSHOTS OF THE NEXT TEST EVEN BEFORE IT HAPPENS.

Bradman's bat hurled at Larwood.

Bradman getting sock on jaw from Larwood.

Australian Government considers cable from M.C.C. to say that biting is cricket and advising play-the-game-sir.

Fieldsmen stumping Bradman with himself.

Jardine bites Woodfull.

STOP PRESS – Australia declares war.

Sutcliffe, who both scored hundreds in the second innings of the match.

From 1926, or more correctly from 1928 when he first appeared in a Test match, England *v* Australia cricket was dominated for the next two decades by the rise of Donald Bradman. During the 1928–9 series he scored his first hundred in his third Test, aged twenty, and another in the last Test

AUSTRALIAN CIRCUMSTANCES
ALTER CASES
Tom Webster
1932. *Daily Mail*

of the series. When he first came to England in 1930 his performance – and its effect – was scintillating. His seven Test innings included scores of 131, 254, 334 (setting a new Test record and including 309 in a day, still a Test record) and 232.

The advent of Bradman seemed to change the whole complexion of Test cricket. His scoring was so prolific and regular that it posed insurmountable problems for any side hoping to beat Australia. It was primarily through his determination to diminish Bradman's effectiveness that Douglas Jardine, England captain for the next series in 1932–3, devised the tactic of Bodyline, which was to cause the first and most serious cricketing crisis between the two countries.

The essence of Bodyline – or leg theory – was fast, short-pitched bowling at the batsman rather than at his wicket, with a ring of close leg-side fielders to take any catches offered as the batsman attempted to defend himself. In his fast bowlers, especially Harold Larwood and his partner Bill Voce, Jardine had the ideal pair to carry out his plan. Bodyline caused immediate hostility in Australia, but when their batsmen began to be injured and players and spectators alike sensed that the tactic was a carefully organized campaign by Jardine, it was not long before their anger boiled over, both at matches and in the famous cable of complaint sent to the MCC, which took the row to its highest level.

Whether Bodyline was 'unsportsmanlike' and dangerous, as the Australians complained, or whether, as the MCC maintained, the Australians were exaggerating and making a storm in a teacup, it was a gift for cartoonists, providing a never-ending daily supply of subjects and stories for weeks on end. Low's cartoon also illustrates the newsworthy importance that the affair gained, for it was not often that cricket provided the subject matter (rather than, as was often the case, the setting) either for him or for any other political cartoonist.

If Bodyline attracted the pens of political cartoonists such as Low it was an irresistible opportunity for England's foremost sporting cartoonist, Tom Webster, which he exploited to the full. In December 1932 – during the First Test, when the Australian protests had already started – he produced a cartoon with a running commentary which put the situation into proportion for many Englishmen by arguing that Larwood was no worse than Gregory and McDonald had been under Armstrong's direction in 1921.

KEEPING IT CLEAN
Tom Webster
1933. *Daily Mail*

The cartoon shows Webster at his best; it is packed with different images and little humorous asides as well as the main theme. In addition, the spontaneity and freshness of both drawings and comment point to the speed at which Webster usually worked, which was one of the keys to his success. Initially speed was necessary to meet deadlines, but it was not long before Webster realized to what extent it was to his advantage, giving his cartoons a fluidity and compelling pace. There are many accounts of how quickly he worked, capped – as one would expect – by the artist himself: 'Last week I was putting on my golf shoes at 2.20 with the cartoon not started. I got an idea, and at 2.35 the ink was dry on the paper. That cartoon took me seven minutes.'

A few weeks later, in January 1933, in the middle of the Adelaide Test which was the flash-point of the crisis, Webster produced his most famous cartoon of the whole affair: 'Let's Have a Nice Game of Cricket, or a possible scene at Brisbane in the next Test match'. It would certainly have amused *Daily Mail* readers, but it also illustrated the level that hostilities had reached.

When England next returned to Australia after the Bodyline

KANGAROO SOUP
'I've been in it twice myself, dear boys, and I know.'
E. H. Shepard (1879–1976)
1937

Shepard first drew for *Punch* in 1907 and became the chief cartoonist in 1945.

tour, in 1936–7, they were without either Douglas Jardine or Harold Larwood. Not only had Australia's visit to England in 1934 done much to restore relations to normality, but this time England was captained by the far more conciliatory G. O. Allen – a fast bowler who had played on the Bodyline tour but refused to fall in with Jardine's tactics.

Under Allen England won the first two Tests, but the tide turned against them during the Third Test which Australia won convincingly, going on to win the last two. Chief engineer of their success was Don Bradman: 270 in the Third Test at Melbourne, followed by 212 at Adelaide and 169 at Melbourne again in the last. Therefore it is hardly surprising that in his cartoon about the Third Test entitled 'Kangaroo Soup', the *Punch* artist E. H. Shepard shows Bradman stirring a cauldron containing Allen, along with Walter Hammond and Hedley Verity.

Shepard's drawing captures the event in question but its style and humour are both somewhat bland and flat – disappointingly so considering that here was the artist who drew the magical characters of *Winnie the Pooh* and *The Wind in the Willows*. Shepard produced a number of the weekly political 'cuts' for *Punch* between the wars, but in both humour and technique they did not compare with his smaller sketch cartoons drawn for the magazine which were far more akin to the immortal animals he created.

If the animosity of Bodyline has fortunately never again soured the cricketing relations between England and Australia, aggressive fast bowling has often given successive confrontations great spice. In 1972 Roy Ullyett highlighted this with a cartoon showing England dishing out the treatment to the unfortunate Australians (*see page 109*). When he was working for the *Daily Express* Ullyett once remarked that 'anyone who wades through to the back page of a newspaper *deserves* a laugh', and his work always contained the instantaneous note of humour evident here. In his caption, a comment by the non-striking batsman, Ullyett echoes the sentiments of Webster in 1933 – that for the Australians, bowling bouncers was all right so long as they were doing it: 'That sort of delivery might well serve to strengthen his belief that the bouncer should have been banned the moment Lindwall and Miller retired.'

In fact, apart from the freak performance by Bob Massie at Lord's when he took 16 for 137, the bowling in the series was dominated by Dennis Lillee, making his first appearance in England, with 31 wickets in the five Tests – a record for an Australian in England. It is Lillee who provides the subject for a pair of cartoons by Ralph Steadman, done at the Centenary Test in Melbourne in 1977 (*see page 110*), when his bowling was decisive; eleven wickets in the two innings ensuring Australia's victory.

From the chilling humour of Steadman, John Jensen's cartoon of the hysterical level of media interest at the beginning of England's tour of Australia in 1986–7 brings an altogether more light-hearted touch, at the same time as making a telling comment upon the modern game (*see page 111*). As well as the straight coverage of actual cricket, a Test series today involves a fierce spotlight upon the players from both press and television which is usually detrimental to its smooth and happy progress. Despite this, however, and the threat to the popularity of five-day Tests from the one-day game, it is certain that of all Test competitions the most likely to continue to be fought competitively and to arouse the most patriotic sentiments among spectators are those for the Ashes, between England and Australia.

CHAPTER EIGHT

Lord's and the MCC

After two hundred years of the MCC and only thirty-odd years less at Lord's, both club and ground have an unshakable air of establishment and authority. This is hardly surprising, as for most of the two centuries they have been central to the game's development. Until the 1960s the MCC's hand was firm and unquestioned on the rudder. Lord's became the most hallowed ground in the world, and to play there the ultimate thrill for any cricketer who had the opportunity to do so; wherever he came from, to watch there was a pastime quite different from spectating anywhere else. Many people have recorded their feelings about Lord's, including the Australian all-rounder Keith Miller whom one would not normally think of as given to sentimental utterings. His comment was used by Tony Lewis in *Double Century* to illustrate the mystique of Lord's: 'Tradition, that's what it's called. Every time I walked up those sprig-scarred steps of the Pavilion I knew I was in the very same footsteps of W. G. Grace.'

As in any similar situation, the prestige of Lord's and the MCC and their high-profile role in cricket's evolution have involved constant exposure and regular comment and analysis, both critical and humorous. This is partly because within the world of cricket – and often beyond – they have always been newsworthy, and partly through an enjoyment of lampooning or making fun of anyone set up on a pedestal of authority. Pronouncements by the MCC, matches at Lord's and the leading characters involved have provided humorous artists with a constant source of material which has unfailingly had an eager audience.

The leading characters in the story of Lord's and the MCC have been a diverse mixture. The first two, Thomas Lord who found and set out the ground and William Ward, player and banker who bought the lease from Lord as the latter was threatening to sell the site for development, were two quite different men, as again was the man who took on the lease from Ward in 1835, James Henry Dark.

Dark, who remained proprietor of Lord's for the next thirty years, was an entrepreneur determined to improve the place in any way possible: as a cricket ground, as a club for MCC members and as somewhere with appeal to a paying general public. Sheep were brought in to graze the grass, the playing area was later drained at Dark's personal expense, the Pavilion was given gas lighting, and a billiard room and real tennis court were built. For non-cricketing sporting activities a running track was laid and pony racing was held.

There seemed few limits to Dark's ingenuity when it came to staging events to draw the crowds and many, such as an

CRICKET SKETCHES
James Dark. (1795–?)
c. 1840

invitation to a group of American Red Indians to camp on the ground and perform at baseball, archery and dancing, displayed a keen sense of humour which was confirmed by the series of cricket cartoons which Dark drew and published around 1840. The cartoons were a series of eleven showing 'stick' cricketers in different postures of the game, each with its own complementary caption. If their extreme simplicity disguises the skill in their drawing, the wit of the artist is immediately evident.

Towards the end of his proprietorship of Lord's Dark made it clear that he hoped the MCC would buy the freehold. When, however, it came up for sale in 1860, they declined to do so and it went to a Mr Moses for £7000. The next few years saw the MCC widely criticized, with many people suggesting that it should be replaced as the body of authority over the game by a cricket parliament, and although they did take on the lease from Dark when he left in 1864, the club must have felt threatened.

The situation was put to rights by the man appointed MCC Secretary in 1863, R. A. Fitzgerald (*see page 112*). 'Bob' Fitzgerald was twenty-nine at the time and his main assets were ceaseless energy and keen wit, both of which were to help him in stirring the more entrenched members of the MCC – and especially the members of the committee – from their reactionary lethargy. It was Fitzgerald's ceaseless activity and the subsequent benefits for the MCC which led him to be made the first paid, permanent secretary five years after his initial appointment. As a cricketer Fitzgerald's credentials were more than respectable: Harrow, Cambridge (a Blue two years) and subsequently MCC and IZ. He was well known as an attacking batsman and his most celebrated hit put the ball over the tennis court at Lord's and out of the ground into St John's Wood Road. His first major achievement as Secretary was to persuade the MCC committee that the club should buy the freehold they had passed up a few years earlier. In 1866 they paid £18,000, substantially more than the price of 1860, but at last the club was immovably rooted in its ground.

Fitzgerald's determination to secure the MCC's position and reputation at the top of cricket were assisted decisively by the fact that his years as Secretary (1863–76) saw the rise to fame of W. G. Grace, a dedicated MCC player and supporter. Together they made a formidable partnership, not least in appearance as is shown in a pair of caricatures which hang in

CRICKET AT LORD'S: THE
LUNCHEON INTERVAL
By our Special Instantaneous
Photographic Caricaturist
Harry Furniss
1891. *Punch*

the Pavilion at Lord's. Fitzgerald sported as impressive a beard as the doctor himself and is depicted wearing a pillbox hat in the colours of IZ which was later replaced by the modern peaked cap worn by Grace – his with the orange and yellow hoops of the MCC.

It was during the period of renaissance at Lord's, masterminded by Fitzgerald and boosted and publicized by W.G.'s performance and charisma, that the ground's social importance – focusing upon the three major matches established earlier in the century, Eton *v* Harrow, Gents *v* Players and Oxford *v* Cambridge – became both significant and assured. Membership of the club had always carried a certain social cachet, but now high society itself was being attracted to Lord's, to attend these senior matches. At Lord's Week in July, when Oxford *v* Cambridge was followed by Eton *v* Harrow, the atmosphere and style were similar to that of any other of the leading events of the summer season.

In July 1891 Harry Furniss produced a cartoon for *Punch*
entitled 'Cricket at Lord's, the Luncheon Interval', which
vividly depicts a typical scene at Lord's during the summer. As
Furniss makes clear, not only was high society attracted, but a
rich cross-section of other classes, many of whom came to
look at the members of society, on display and decked out in

CRICKET LOVERS
James Thorpe
1927

their finery. Like the woman of the same period who remarked that she had attended every day of Royal Ascot and not seen a horse, there were those who spent a day at Lord's without seeing a ball bowled. For many ladies the right hat was more important than the right result.

The elegance of Lord's crowds probably reached a peak during the late Victorian and Edwardian eras, a time when dressing up was an obsessive pastime of the upper classes. It survived into the inter-war period, as James Thorpe shows in a sketch cartoon of 1920s fashion, whose caption, 'The Cricket Lovers', makes the humorous point that cricket – or at least watching it – was a low priority for the immaculately dressed couple promenading below the Grandstand at Lord's. In another cartoon Thorpe makes fun of the socially unacceptable character of The Oval compared with Lord's, showing in a picture called 'Those Who Never Go to The Oval' a selection of upper-class or distinguished individuals for whom the only possible place to attend would have been Lord's.

Of all the major matches at Lord's none attracted a more exclusive and elegant crowd than Eton *v* Harrow, the senior fixture in that it was first played in 1805 – the year before the initial Gents *v* Players match. The carriages around the boundary, proud mothers and sisters and lavish picnics during the luncheon interval – all helped to give the fixture the

PEOPLE WHO NEVER GO TO THE OVAL
James Thorpe

appearance of a garden party as well as a cricket match. At the same time, the absurdity that a cricket match between school-boys should attract such attention – however senior the schools and however many of the players would later be seen performing for Oxford and Cambridge, the Gentlemen or possibly even England – was not lost on many observers for whom Eton *v* Harrow came round as an annual gem of humorous possibilities not be missed.

It is absolutely suitable that one of the most exquisite cartoons of the Eton *v* Harrow match should have been drawn by George du Maurier, *Punch*'s outstanding social cartoonist of the Victorian era. Du Maurier drew 'A Reminiscence of Lord's Cricket Ground' in 1878. In sepia pen and ink, it is complete in its complex detail and as a piece of social obser-vation, in a style that du Maurier developed to a masterly

A REMINISCENCE OF LORD'S
CRICKET GROUND
Charles (post-prandially): 'Aw! –
Awfully jolly, if it weren't for the
cricket, ain't it?'
Fred (ditto): 'Yaas. Cricket's awfully
slow. If it were only rounders now -
or skittles, you know!'
George du Maurier
1878. *Punch*

The Eton *v* Harrow match was a subject tailor-made for the pen of George du Maurier, with members of society lunching on their carriages drawn up around the boundary. The atmosphere is so languid that it verges on boredom.

ALLY SLOPER AT ETON v
HARROW
W. G. Baxter
Ally Sloper's Half Holiday

degree. The detail – the gentlemen in their frock-coats, curly-brimmed toppers and gleaming top-boots, the ladies perched upon the carriages in full, high-necked dresses and huge, gloriously adorned hats, the liveried coachman packing up the wicker picnic basket – brings the scene immediately to life.

The execution of du Maurier's cartoon is as stylish as his subjects, but for another Victorian cartoonist, W. G. Baxter, and his main character, Ally Sloper, neither stylishness nor subtlety was necessary. For them Eton *v* Harrow was a God-given opportunity to poke a bit of fun at the toffs and for the benefit of the readers of *Ally Sloper's Half Holiday* Ally himself regularly attended the match, along with a selection of his family and friends. Here he is dressed up in Eton uniform, hideously absurd and yet appealing – certainly to addicts of the halfpenny weekly – compared with the stuffy-looking society members passing behind him.

Left
THE ETON BOY COLLAPSES
Tom Webster
1925. *Daily Mail*

A later cartoonist for whom Eton *v* Harrow often provided the opportunity for a bit of fun was Tom Webster, not least in 1925 when he produced 'The Eton Boy Collapses, or The Harrow Child Gets into the Picture for the First Time Since 1908'. Eton's domination of the fixture had been unbroken since that date and here at last, with an Eton batting collapse, Harrow had the chance to reset the balance. In the event, they failed and had to wait until 1939 before they won again.

Right
THE MOTHER WHO
KISSED HER SON
AT LORD'S
H. M. Bateman
c. 1920

The antics of Webster's two boys could easily have been those of any number of the members of the two schools, for whom attendance was compulsory and for whom the outcome of the match was of dire importance. Not only for the boys was it important: when Harrow finally won in 1939, John Christie, who for many years had been a master at Eton, went on to the stage of his private opera-house at Glyndebourne in the interval to announce the devastating news – not, as most of the audience expected, that some dreadful development had taken place in the build-up to the Second World War, but that Eton had been defeated for the first time in 31 years.

At an event of such social distinction as Eton *v* Harrow the observation of correct etiquette and behaviour was of paramount importance. For those who failed to conform the penalty was disgrace and acute embarrassment, as illustrated by the master of the social gaffe, H. M. Bateman, in his cartoon 'The Mother Who Kissed Her Son at Lord's'. To the glee of the assembled onlookers, the offending mother is quite oblivious of her ghastly blunder, but there is no doubt that the poor son – who is all too aware of the consequences – would never again be able to lift his head at school.

Since the Second World War the social importance of Eton *v* Harrow and the two other traditional Lord's matches has declined dramatically. Whereas right up until 1939 the ground was nearly always full for all three, now only a few hundred at most turn up for Eton *v* Harrow and the University Match, and the Gents *v* Players fixture was played for the last time in 1962, a few months before the formal distinction was abolished. Today Eton *v* Harrow has been reduced to a one-day match and it seems likely that, despite its historic tradition, its days at Lord's are now numbered.

Quite different to the social priorities of these fixtures has been a question of basic importance regarding the actual playing of matches at Lord's – the state of the wicket and the playing area as a whole, which have been regularly criticized (at least until very recently) since the early days. The shortcomings of the wicket were one of the major problems Fitzgerald had to face, and probably the one he made least progress in improving. In his day, when it was crucial to try to attract the leading players to Lord's in order to bring in large crowds, the criticisms of the pitch by these players and their

THE LORD'S WICKET
Roy Ullyett
Daily Express

Ullyett once remarked about his work as a newspaper sports cartoonist, 'anyone who can read through to the back page of the newspaper deserves a laugh'.

consequent widespread refusal to play at Lord's were a considerable disadvantage.

The two main peculiarities of the ground are the pro-
nounced slope of six feet six inches from the Grandstand side
to the Tavern side, and the 'ridge', whose existence many
contest but which is supposed to be the course of an old drain,
running straight across the square and – if hit by an accurate
bowler – causing the ball to lift sharply at batsmen at the
Pavilion End.

Over the years there have been regular cartoons on the
theme of the one produced by Roy Ullyett for the *Daily
Express*, at a time when the ground was under scrutiny for
some reason or other. In three sketches with accompanying
comments by the 'experts' Ullyett wittily exaggerates the
nature and extent of the problem. 1. '*Sir Edmund Hillary*
(conqueror of Everest): "There is no reason why cricket
should not continue provided players take oxygen on the
heights at the Pavilion End."' 2. '*A Mining Engineer*: "Play
is possible. The air is not too foul. My canary only passed out
in the deep parts."' 3. '*A Very Regular Taverner*: "It
confirms what I've always said. After 14 pints the wicket
waves up and down."' As a postscript Ullyett adds his own
conclusion: 'In future the groundsman will inquire of the
captain taking second knock, "Sir, do you require the light
roller, the heavy roller or a bulldozer?"'

However much the Lord's wicket may have been criticized
over the years it is certain that no MCC member, past or
present, would find it easy to agree with such criticism – or,
indeed, any other to do with club or ground. The element of
elitism about members of the MCC which has probably
always been there leads some people today to regard the club,
secure in its citadel of Lord's, as a bastion of conservatism,
tradition and privilege, all maintained to an archaic degree.

The members – or at least, the more extreme ones – view the
situation differently. They are convinced of their hereditary
superiority in the cricketing world and if the MCC no longer
runs the game, it's a damn shame and we would not be
in today's mess if they still did. Sponsorship, the one-day
game and most contemporary players are viewed with deep
suspicion. Lord's they regard as their domain which is occasionally invaded by the common herd, and both the ground
as a whole and the inner sanctum of the Pavilion are a shrine
whose glories are protected by protocol and regulations.

TIE!
Jak
1975. *Evening Standard*

Of course, people like that do not really exist, but it is imagination along such lines which has led to the archetypal MCC member being invariably depicted in cartoons as an apoplectic colonel, wearing his MCC tie and blazer with gleaming regimental buttons, grasping a large gin and tonic, his moustache twitching with rage at some travesty being related.

No one has drawn the members better than Jak of the *Evening Standard*, who has often caricatured them when appearing to be at their most entrenched. On one occasion in 1975 he showed some poor innocent who had not familiarized himself with the rule that members are required to wear a tie in the Pavilion. The scene provided Jak with the opportunity for great hilarity at the members' expense, showing them preserving form to a ridiculous extent.

Such a position might be bad form but it is, after all, remediable. Far more serious was a frontal assault on the prestige and good judgement of the MCC which came in 1983, when it was maintained in a national newspaper that a large number of the paintings which had been bequeathed to the MCC by Sir Jeremiah Coleman, and which formed a major part of the club's art collection, were fakes. The MCC's authority over the game may have declined dramatically since the 1960s, but the importance of its position as the custodian of the game's heritage has risen correspondingly and such an attack was a weighty blow. Again it provided Jak with a situation to be exploited.

The more unhappy incidents during England's winter tours of 1987–8 were just the sort of thing to incur the wrath of traditional MCC members, and in a cartoon for *Punch* which

FAKES
'I always thought it was a fake, it's nothing like Boycott's stance at the crease.'
Jak
1983. *The Standard*

THE MEMBERS' VERDICT
John Jensen
1988. *Punch*

appeared shortly before the team's return from New Zealand John Jensen illustrated the punishment they would prescribe, given the opportunity. But although the MCC is still closely involved in the running of the game it no longer has direct authority over tours abroad or Test series at home, and in the event heads did not roll.

Humorous jests about the MCC and its members and cartoons and caricatures of them are part of life, but what the club's more dedicated critics – convinced that it is indeed a regiment of old die-hards – miss is the part that the MCC has played in the progress and education of the game of cricket from its eighteenth-century childhood through two hundred years. At its best the club's role has been avuncular and tutorial, a position inevitably involving the prescription of restraint and, at times, firm discipline as well as encouragement. The standards of the game – at least those worth preserving – are largely those given to it by the MCC. Today the MCC may appear to have stepped down from active involvement in the management of cricket, but it is still a powerful force and a body which has survived so well for so long that it is more than likely to continue to do so.

Index

(Page references in italics refer to illustrations)